Elements of Pantheism

Paul Harrison

D1557298

Llumina Press

ISBN: 1-59526-317-9
Printed in the United States of America by Llumina Press

Second edition © Paul Harrison 2004
First edition published in 1999 by Element Books, Shaftesbury, Dorset.

Note on illustrations:

The front cover is from a Hubble Telescope photo of the galaxy M100 with a spiral shell superimposed. Many natural forms such as spirals, radials, branching, networks, waves and so on are found in living and non-living materials and at many different scales. The juxtaposition, which is the symbol of the World Pantheist Movement, emphasizes the unity and community of the organic and inorganic worlds.

The chapter headings are high contrast renderings of individual snowflakes originally photographed by Wilson Alwyn Bentley (1865-1931), illustrating the astonishing diversity and complexity that arises spontaneously from a few simple rules of crystal geometry.

Elements of Pantheism

Contents

1. What is Pantheism and is it for you?

ARE YOU A PANTHEIST? Do you feel a deep sense of peace and belonging and wonder in the midst of nature, in a forest, by the ocean, or on a mountain top?

Are you speechless with awe when you look up at the sky on a clear moonless night and see the Milky Way strewn with stars as thick as sand on a beach?

When you see breakers crashing on a rocky shore, or hear wind rustling in a poplar's leaves, are you uplifted by the energy and creativity of existence?

Finally, do you find it difficult to imagine anything more worthy of your deepest reverence than the beauty of nature or the power of the universe?

If you answered yes to these questions, then you are almost certainly a Pantheist.

In this chapter we will look at a brief outline of pantheism before going into more detail.

What is Pantheism?

The word Pantheism derives from the Greek words pan (="all") and theos (="God"). Thus, Pantheism means: All is God. In essence, Pantheism holds that the Universe as a whole is worthy of the deepest reverence, and that only the Universe and Nature are worthy of that degree of reverence.

The statement "Nature is my god" is perhaps the simplest way of summarizing the core Pantheist belief, with the word god here meaning not some supernatural being but the object of deepest personal reverence. Pantheism is a spiritual path that reveres and cares for nature. A spiritual path that joyously accepts this life as our only life, and this earth as our only paradise, if we look after it. Pantheism revels in the beauty of nature and the night sky, and is full of wonder at their mystery and power.

Pantheism believes that all things are linked in a profound unity. All things have a common origin and a common destiny. All things are interconnected and interdependent. In life and in death we humans are an inseparable part of this unity, and in realizing this we can find our joy and our peace.

A Gallery of "isms"

Theism: Belief in one personal judging creator God who transcends the world, and who may or may not be immanent in it.

Panentheism: Belief in a personal creator God who transcends the world, but is also intimately present and active in the world and in each of us.

Pantheism: Profound religious reverence for the Universe/Nature.

Atheism: Disbelief in any supernatural deity.

Humanism: A positive atheistic philosophy stressing human responsibility for our ethical choices.

Polytheism: Belief in and worship of many gods.

Paganism (modern): Nature-oriented form of polytheism, usually revering Goddess and God, and sometimes other deities. Paganism may involve literal belief in those deities, or just symbolic use of them as aids to revere Nature.

Pantheism is among the oldest of religious beliefs. It can be dated back to at least the sixth or seventh centuries BC, when the Hindu Upanishads were written, and the Greek philosopher Heraclitus flourished. Pantheism, of one kind or another, came to dominate the ancient world East and West.

The spread of Christianity and Islam forced Pantheism underground for some 1200 years, but by the nineteenth century it was beginning to regain some of its old prominence. It was the dominant belief of many philosophers and poets from Wordsworth and Goethe to Hegel and Walt Whitman.

The bleak first half of the twentieth century pushed Pantheism into the background again, but today it is enjoying a new renaissance in Natural Pantheism, nature-oriented paganism, deep ecology, philosophical Taoism, Zen Buddhism, and religious forms of Humanism and atheism.

All Pantheists feel the same profound reverence for the Universe/Nature, but different Pantheists use different forms of language to express this reverence. Traditionally, Pantheism has made use of theistic-sounding words like "God," but in basically non-theistic ways - pantheists do not believe in a supernatural creator personal god who will judge us all after death.

Modern pantheists fall into two distinct groups in relation to language: some avoid words such as God or divine, because this makes listeners think in terms of traditional concepts of God that may be very misleading. Others are quite comfortable using these words, but when they use them they don't mean the same thing that conventional theists mean. If they say the Universe is God, they don't mean that the Universe is identical with the deity in the Bible or the Koran. They mean that for them the Universe has the status of a god and awakens in them at least some of the feelings of awe and wonder and love and acceptance and gratitude that Jews, Christians and Moslems feel towards their God.

The Irish writer John Toland first used the word Pantheist in 1705, and defined it as a person who believes "in no other eternal being but the universe."

By and large the modern definition of Pantheism is still close to Toland's. Here are a few authoritative modern versions:

- The religious belief or philosophical theory that God and the Universe are identical (implying a denial of the personality and transcendence of God); the doctrine that God is everything and everything is God. [Oxford English Dictionary]
- A doctrine that equates God with the forces and laws of the universe. [Merriam Webster Collegiate]
- The doctrine that the universe conceived of as a whole is God and, conversely, that there is no God but the combined substance, forces, and laws that are manifested in the existing universe. [Encyclopaedia Britannica]

Why do people become Pantheists?

Most Pantheists in Western countries today were not reared as Pantheists, but as Christians, Jews, Muslims, atheists or agnostics. So what made them become Pantheists?

Usually they had grown unhappy with the religions or beliefs they were brought up in. In the case of Christianity, for example, they could no longer accept the claims of impossible miracles, or logical conundrums such as a God who is both three and one, or a Saviour who is both human and divine.

Many Pantheists also feel that the traditional religions are too oriented towards invisible beings and realms, and not enough towards the real world we inhabit, towards this present life, and towards the body.

Dissatisfaction with established religions drove people on long spiritual journeys, often through many alternative beliefs, in search of alternatives, testing out the many forms of Buddhism, paganism, Humanism or simple atheism.

But in all of them there was still an unsatisfied yearning for spirituality: the need for a system of beliefs and practices that relate us emotionally to nature and the universe, that tell us of our place as a member of them. They felt the need to go beyond Atheism, which simply denies the existence of a personal creator God and takes no positive positions about how we should live our lives or how we should feel about the Universe/Nature.

When people join the World Pantheist Movement they are asked to say why they became Pantheists. Here's just a small selection of their comments:

> *As early as I can remember, the trees, the wind, and the rivers spoke with greater reverberation than my parents or the elders of the church. The sense I have always known that I am not separate from the beetles, the irises, the rocks, the deer has given me hope and inner peace and strength in times of need. HC.*

> *After trying every religion I could find, I still never feel closer to anything truly divine than when I am, without ideas, being in nature. All these other schools of thought - they only add unnecessary flourishes to what is already enough. TO.*

> *My understanding of these things has gone beyond the normal `atheistic' mode. There is a spiritual/emotional side to life - that is part of what it means to be human. I feel awe and reverence when I watch a sunset or catch a glimpse of a kingfisher. AM*

> *I can't picture God as a being floating around on a cloud, controlling the earth, but I can picture a supreme being as nature and everything around me. LG.*

> *I ended up with the philosophical connectiveness to the universe without the supernaturalism. Guess what that is? Pantheism. EM.*

> *I can not trust a god that needs to be reminded of his/her superiority all the time. I and my friends have always stood apart in our belief that the Earth is our Mother and that Nature itself was our beginning and end. RP.*

I cannot accept the idea of an anthropomorphic God, but at the same time, I cannot agree with the desolate landscape of true atheism. BW

I have a strong belief in the overwhelming power of Nature, and that the Power of Nature is the only power that collectively is bigger than me or my species. HD.

A form of spirituality for our modern age

The world's major religions originated in times very different from today: superstitious times when science was rudimentary and education limited to a small elite. They were also times of high mortality from wars and epidemics, when life was cheap and dreams of a paradise after death seemed tempting.

Science and education have made life more difficult for the gods of traditional religions. Once the idea of God provided a handy catch-all explanation for deep questions such as how the universe began, how life and mind arose. But today science is providing convincing answers for all of these, forcing the idea of a creator God to retreat to an area outside of space and time.

Education has taught people to think independently and critically. It's difficult for educated people today to believe in dogma or miracles merely because a parent, a priest or an ancient book proclaims it. People seek for sounder foundations, and ask for harder evidence of what religions claim. If that evidence does not satisfy reason, more and more people chose to reject religions of every kind.

These trends have favoured the spread of scepticism, agnosticism and atheism. Yet none of these positions are fully satisfying. The first two admit that they have no answers, while atheism provides only a single negative position: that there is no God.

Yet there is still a deep human need for the experience of spirituality. Most people have a sense that there is something greater than the self or than the human race, a need for belonging and context. They feel a need for answers to the deepest questions that science cannot answer: questions about the central values of our lives, the anchoring points for our being, and the ethical guidelines for our actions.

Pantheism is in a unique position to satisfy these spiritual needs, without sacrificing any of the critical and empirical spirit that education fosters. It is well suited to the scientific age, the space age and the environmental age we are living in.

- Pantheism accepts and affirms life joyously. It does not regard this life as a waiting room or a staging post on the way to a better existence after death.

- Pantheism has a healthy and positive attitude to sex and life in the body.
- Pantheism teaches reverence and love for nature. Nature was not created for us to use or abuse - nature created us, we are an inseparable part of her, and we have a duty of care towards her.
- Pantheism is uniquely adapted to the space age. The Hubble telescope has revealed the vastness, power, creativity and violence of the universe. We need an idea of divinity in keeping with this new knowledge.
- Pantheism does not simply co-exist uncomfortably with science: it fully embraces science as part of the human exploration of the divine universe.

What Pantheism is not

Pantheism is often confused with several other contrasting or parallel religious belief systems.

Let's take a look first at what Pantheism is not.

Pantheism is not theism.

Theism (from Greek *theos* = God) is the belief in an all-powerful, omniscient, thinking God who created the universe and watches personally over each one of us. He may be present to the universe in carrying out his actions or sustaining things in existence, but essentially he is thought of as infinite and eternal, beyond space and time. This is the God of the central traditions of Judaism, Christianity, and Islam.

Pantheism does have its own "God" (though many Pantheists choose not to use the word), but this god is the Universe itself. Some Pantheists such as the Stoics have believed that the Universe has a collective soul or a purpose in its evolution. But many simply revere the physical universe that science and our senses reveal to us, just as it is.

Critics of Pantheism often suggest that in this case God is simply an extra and unnecessary name for the Universe. However, when Pantheists refer to the Universe as their god, what they really mean is that they feel the same profound sense of awe and reverence that other believers feel towards their gods. To call the Universe "god" or "divine" is not at all meaningless. Although it does not tell us anything extra about the Universe itself, it expresses the powerful emotions that Pantheists feel towards the Universe. It is similar to using the word "beauty" of a natural landscape. "Beauty" is not just another word for the landscape, it expresses our positive aesthetic feelings towards it.

Pantheism is not panentheism.

The word panentheism was first used in 1874, and derives from the Greek words pan-en-theos, meaning "All in God." God is still seen as the supreme all-powerful creator and personal judge, but he is no longer wholly separate from his creation. Part of him transcends space and time, so he is greater than the Universe and precedes the Universe. But at the same time he is present throughout the Universe, in every atom and every living thing. Many Jews, Christians and Muslims are panentheists - indeed none of these religions believe in a totally distant and wholly separate God.

Pantheism, by contrast, does not believe in a God who even partly transcends time and space. The central focus of reverence is the Universe itself, right here, right now in this present time, all around us and in us. We are each part of the awe-inspiring whole and it is part of us.

The American humorist Ambrose Bierce cleverly caught the difference with panentheism in *The Devil's Dictionary*. He defined Pantheism as "the belief that everything is God, as opposed to the belief that God is everything."

Pantheism is not polytheism.

Many people confuse Pantheism with polytheism. Polytheism (from Greek poly = "many" and theos = "god") means belief in many gods, as in ancient Greece and Rome, the Celtic and Nordic worlds, and in popular Indian and Chinese religion.

The confusion arises from the word "pantheon" which means the collection of all the gods of a nation, or the temple in Rome dedicated to the gods of all the nations.

But part of the problem lies with dictionaries. They often list a second meaning for Pantheism as the acceptance or worship of *all* the gods of *all* the nations. This meaning started life as an error of usage which crept into the mother of all modern English dictionaries, the massive Oxford English Dictionary.

The OED had literally hundreds of volunteers searching for and reading material from every period in the history of English. Some of the examples they found showed a different usage of the word Pantheism, to mean the indiscriminate acceptance of all the gods of all the nations, such as existed in the later Roman Empire, when Rome absorbed the religions of many of its conquered nations.

The first recorded example of the word Pantheism with this meaning dates from 1837 - well over a century later than Toland's first use of the word "Pantheist." But once it got into the great OED, it filtered from there into many other modern dictionaries.

This second meaning is very rare in print today. Most modern encyclo-paedias, and all textbooks on religion and philosophy, deal only with the first meaning, equating the Universe with God.

The second meaning is in direct contradiction to the first. Indeed the sec-ond meaning is not even normal polytheism. Polytheism usually worships the gods of a particular culture, and different polytheisms have different sets of gods - but Pantheism in this meaning worships or accepts all the gods of all cultures on earth.

Neither polytheism nor Pantheism in this second meaning are compatible with Pantheism as normally understood. It is not logically possible to believe in literally in many gods, and at the same time to believe that the Universe is the only thing worthy of the deepest religious reverence.

Pantheism and its near neighbours

There are some religious orientations that Pantheism is close to and overlaps with, but is not identical to. These include atheism, Humanism, and paganism. It is perfectly possible to combine Pantheism with any of these views, and many people do.

Pantheism and Atheism

Atheism is disbelief in God, more specifically disbelief in any sort of per-sonal, thinking being with supernatural powers, as found in theism, panentheism or polytheism. The word stems from the Greek *a-theos,* meaning "without God."

The nineteenth century German philosopher Schopenhauer once remarked that Pantheism was simply a polite form of atheism. In one sense he was right. Pantheism is atheistic towards the gods of all traditional religions. It does not believe in any separate creator, or in a personal judging God. Many Pantheists of a physicalist bent agree with atheists that all phenomena are a part of na-ture. They do not believe there are any supernatural beings or spirit realms, and that if any currently unexplained phenomena such as extra-sensory per-ception should eventually be established as real, they will operate through natural physical forces.

But there are differences. Atheism does not claim to be a coherent philoso-phy, religion or way of life. It has only one unifying belief: that there is no personal creator God. Modern atheism is usually based on respect for logic, reason and evidence and to that extent endorses these values. But beyond that. atheism does not make any positive statements. It does not involve any particu-lar way of viewing the universe. It is quite possible for an atheist to regard the universe as absurd and hostile and human life as depressingly meaningless. Clearly, this approach is emotionally very distant from Pantheism.

But many atheists have been uncomfortable with the purely negative. Many have had a profound religious awe and humility towards nature and the universe. As Carl Sagan wrote in *Pale Blue Dot*:

> *A religion old or new, that stressed the magnificence of the universe as revealed by modern science, might be able to draw forth reserves of reverence and awe hardly tapped by the conventional faiths. Sooner or later, such a religion will emerge.*

This sort of approach is sometimes known as positive atheism or religious atheism. It is identical with naturalistic and scientific forms of Pantheism.

A good way of summing up the difference between atheism and Pantheism is that atheism defines what a person does not believe, while Pantheism defines what they do believe and feel.

Pantheism and Humanism

Like Pantheists, humanists have felt the need to go beyond atheism, to develop a set of more positive beliefs about humans and their place in the universe.

The main stress in Humanism has been on human responsibility to choose our own destiny, and to create our own ethical systems without supernatural backing. In recent decades there has been an increasing focus on human responsibility for nature.

Some humanists have recognized the need for a more religious approach, marked by the founding of the Friends of Religious Humanism in 1962. Many humanists recognize the need for religious ceremonies to mark births, weddings and deaths and have developed non-theist forms of these.

Peter Samson wrote in *Can Humanism be Religious?*:

> *The most meaningful and liveable kind of Humanism is itself a religious way of understanding and living life. It offers a view of [people] and [their] place in the universe that is a religious philosophy...overarching and undergirding it all, there can be a haunting sense of wonder which never leaves one for whom life itself is a mystery and miracle. To be caught up in this sense of wider relatedness, to sense our being connected in live ways with all the world and everyone in it, is the heart dimension of religion, whatever its name.*

This view of religious Humanism is more or less identical with religious atheism and with Natural Pantheism. It has, however, awakened some strong opposition within the Humanist movement, as from leading secular humanist Paul Kurtz:

The term religious Humanism is unfortunate. . . . Often it serves to sneak in some quasi-spiritual and/or transcendental aspect of experience and practice, aping religion.

Paganism and Animism

The word pagan comes from the Latin *paganus*, which originally meant rustic or rural. In religious terms, it came to be used of those people - often country-dwellers - who stuck to traditional polytheism when Christianity became the official religion of the Roman Empire in the fourth century AD. Today the word is loosely used of any non-Christian who practices a polytheistic or nature-based religion. The most common forms of contemporary paganism are Celtic and Nordic.

Many modern pagans proclaim themselves to be Pantheists. "Divinity is immanent is all Nature," Margot Adler wrote in her account of paganism in the United States, *Drawing Down the Moon*, "It is as much within you as without."

Doreen Valiente's Wiccan poem *Charge of the Goddess* expresses this Pantheism beautifully:

> *I who am the beauty of the green earth,*
> *and the white moon among the stars,*
> *and the mystery of the waters,*
> *call unto thy soul:*
> *Arise, and come unto me.*
> *For I am the soul of nature,*
> *who gives life to the universe.*
> *From Me all things proceed,*
> *and unto Me all things must return;*
> *and before My face, beloved of gods and of men,*
> *let thine innermost divine self be*
> *enfolded in the rapture of the infinite.*

Most pagan cults such as Wicca, however, proclaim at least two gods - Goddess and God - and often more. If these gods are taken as real beings with supernatural powers, then this is a form of polytheism. It is not strictly compatible with Pantheism.

But many modern pagans don't take these deities literally. They see them rather as symbols of different aspects of the power and beauty of Nature and the Universe and poetic ways of expressing reverence for Nature. It is quite possible to be this kind of "symbolic" pagan and to be a Pantheist at the same time.

A closely related belief is animism. Animism holds that every living thing, every animal, plant, tree, rock and stream, has its own spirit or divinity within itself that must be respected and revered.

All Pantheists would agree that each individual thing in nature has its own presence - a presence that, if we truly open our senses and hearts - is mysterious, awesome and commanding of deepest respect. However, where animists might see each such being as in some way independent, the Pantheist would see them as members of a larger unity.

Is Pantheism a philosophy or a religion?

Some people claim that Pantheism cannot be regarded as a religion. This is mainly because Pantheism in the West has been most clearly expressed by individual philosophers such as Giordano Bruno or Spinoza. Until recently it has never been organized under its own name. The most numerous school of pantheists in the classical world, the Stoics, were a school of philosophers and did not have any religious ritual.

Another reason is that many people erroneously assume that religions must include belief in a God or gods. Yet textbooks consider Theravada Buddhism as a religion, and in its original form it does not have a God or gods.

Like Buddhism, Pantheism can be regarded as a philosophy of life, or as a spiritual path, or as a religion. The choice is up to the individual, and depends on how deep are that person's feelings for nature and how far pantheism colours their daily life.

Pantheism deals with many of the issues that philosophy deals with. But it also deals with spiritual/religious issues that reach far beyond typical philosophical discussion. It covers the emotional relationship between humans, nature and the universe. It entails a distinctive approach to ethics, stressing human rights and environmental concern. It has inspired celebratory ceremonies and approaches to meditation and mysticism. And in recent years it has begin to organize as a spiritual path.

In the rest of this book we shall examine these elements of Pantheism.

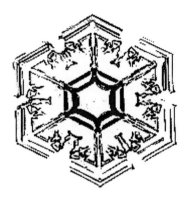

2. The History of Pantheism: Oriental and Classical

PANTHEISM IS A PERENNIAL HERESY that has appeared in every world religion. Less frequently, it has appeared as a philosophy or religion in its own right. But because the word Pantheism was not invented until the early eighteenth century, it rarely appeared under its own name before modern times.

Pantheism has shown up in a number of different varieties, ranging from the simple reverence of the physical universe and nature just as they are, through beliefs in vast cosmic souls, to versions that believe that everything we see is only an illusion concealing a perfect mental unity.

In this chapter and the next we will trace the history of Pantheism in the major religious and philosophical traditions East and West.

Hinduism

Hinduism is not so much a single religion as a vast and diverse collection of related deities, practices and philosophies. Hindus have wide options to choose their own personal gods, or to choose a highly intellectual and philosophical approach. Pantheism runs like a golden thread through the philosophical strand of Hinduism.

The Upanishads, written around 600 BC, were the first philosophical explorations of Hinduism. They describe a cosmic unity linking ourselves and everything around us at mental and physical levels. That unity is called Brahman. In most of the individual Upanishads, Brahman is identical with the world soul, or Atman, and this in turn is identical with the soul of each individual.

As the Chandogya Upanishad expresses it:

Verily this whole world is Brahman. Tranquil, let one worship it as that from which he came forth, as that into which he will be dissolved, as that in which he breathes . . . One should reverence the thought 'I am the World All.'

The Svetasvatara Upanishad puts it more poetically:

Thou art the dark-blue bird and the green parrot with red eyes, Thou hast the lightning as thy child. Thou art the seasons and the seas."

And the Mundaka Upanishad:

Fire is His head; His eyes, the moon and sun; the regions of space, His ears; His voice, the revealed Vedas; Wind, His breath; His heart, the whole world. Out of His feet, the earth. Truly He is the Inner Soul of all.

Perhaps the favourite scripture of educated Hindus is the Bhagavad Gita, written probably in the first or second century AD. A chapter of the immense Indian epic the Mahabharata, it consists of the advice given by the god Vishnu to the hero Arjuna, who is about to fight an army containing his own relatives on the field of Kuruksetra. Vishnu, incarnated as the charioteer Krishna, explains that Arjuna should do his duty and fight in battle. The human soul, which is part of the universal soul, is immortal - therefore no-one is truly slain. If people perform the duties appropriate to their station, without attachment to success or failure, then they cannot be stained by action. The rest of the poem provides the full philosophy underlying this insight.

Himself as in all beings
and all beings as in himself
sees he . . . who sees the same in all . . .
Whoso reveres me as abiding in all things,
adopting the belief in oneness,
though abiding in any possible condition,
that disciplined man abides in Me.
I am taste in water, son of Kunti,
I am light in the moon and sun.

Indian Buddhism

Buddhism began in Northern India in the sixth century BC. In origin it was not at all pantheistic. In the oldest scriptures, written in the Pali language, Buddha teaches that life is essentially suffering. His doctrine is above all a method for avoiding suffering and rebirth into a world of suffering. To do so we must abandon desire and attachment to worldly things, and give up the illusion of having a self. If we achieve this, we can attain nirvana. Nirvana is seen not as some separate divine realm, but simply the permanent cessation of all craving and suffering.

But even in its original form Buddhism contained a germ that could later blossom into pantheistic forms. At the core of nirvana, Buddha saw an "unborn, unoriginated, unmade and unconditioned" ultimate reality. This is not called a god, but it is viewed with the deepest religious reverence and desire for unity, in the same way as pantheists view the Universe and nature. However, Buddha himself still saw the realm of nirvana as being reached by turning one's back on the world of the senses.

Buddha did not create a unified church like that of Roman Catholic Christianity, and divisions soon began to emerge. Between 100 BC and 200 AD new schools grew up which were much less negative about life in this world. These schools became known collectively as the Mahayana or Great Vehicle.

The Mahayana developed the idea of the bodhisattva - the person capable of attaining nirvana in one lifetime, but who voluntarily holds back from this in order to help all others beings towards enlightenment.

Central to the Mahayana approach is the idea of emptiness or *sunyatta*. Buddha himself had taught how all things and all human minds were fleeting and impermanent, totally dependent on other things, having no separate or enduring reality.

The Mahayana thinkers took this idea one step further. If nothing was permanent or separate, then in a sense all things had no persistent reality: everything was unreal, or empty. So we were, right here and now, in the midst of nirvana.

"There is no specifiable difference whatever between nirvana and the everyday world," wrote the great 2nd century Indian philosopher Nagarjuna.

"All things are the perfection of being, infinite perfection, unobscured, unconditioned, " says the Siksammuccaya. "All things are enlightenment . . . Buddha, you have reached the other shore without leaving this one."

Chinese Buddhism

This shift in thinking paved the way for the more life-affirming, world-affirming and pantheistic versions of Buddhism that are found in China and Japan. There are so many different schools, teachers and scriptures that it is impossible here to highlight more than a few.

One of the most pantheistic is the Flower Garland school, known in China as Hua-Yen and in Japan as Kegon. This is based on a vast and extraordinary document known as the *Avatamsaka Sutra*, parts of which are known in Indian, but most only in Chinese versions. It dates from the first or second centuries AD. The sutra paints an infinite cosmos of untold oceans of worlds, and is filled with almost psychedelic imagery of light and jewels and flowers.

The Hua Yen school is fully pantheist. It views the Buddha as a cosmic deity, infinite, eternal, present everywhere, manifesting itself in myriads of forms:

> *The Buddha's body fills the cosmos, appearing before all beings everywhere . . . Buddha has Reality for his body, pure as space itself. All the physical forms that appear he includes in this reality.*

The school taught that ultimate reality and concrete things are identical. All things arise together simultaneously through mutual causation. All things depend on each other and penetrate each other, reflecting each other like jewels. "Every single pore contains everything," wrote the school's Chinese founder, Fa Tsang. Or, as the *Avatamsaka Sutra* puts it, "Even on the tip of a grain of sand, Buddhas as numerous as particles of dust exist."

Zen Buddhism

Probably the best known form of Buddhism on the West today is Zen. It shares Hua-Yen's pantheistic view of reality. "Everything the world contains, grass and trees, bricks and tiles, all creatures, all actions and activities, are nothing but manifestations of the law," said Japanese abbot Muso Kukoshi in 1345.

The following dialogue is reported of Liang Chai, founder of the Tsao Tung (Soto Zen) sect.

> *Monk: What is the mind of an ancient Buddha?*
> *Liang Chai: Just a wall and broken tiles.*
> *Monk: Do they know how to expound the Dharma [law or teaching]?*
> *Liang Chai: They are always expounding the Dharma vigorously without interruption.*

Because the Buddha nature is inherent in everything around us, no laborious rites, no arduous study or poring over the scriptures are needed to realize it. It can be understood in an instant, in a sudden enlightenment known in Japanese as satori. This insight can be brought about by any breaking of the boundaries of ordinary conceptual thinking - hence the apparently absurd mind-puzzles of the Zen koan, or the tales of teachers' physical assaults on pupils to try and shake them up.

Once satori has been achieved, Zen teaches a complete absorption in the ordinary tasks of everyday life by doing them with heightened awareness. "The Buddha Dharma has no room for practice and striving, " said I Hsuan, Chinese founder of the Lin Chi (Rinzai) sect. "You have only to be ordinary and unconcerned, wearing robes, taking food, stooling, passing water, and resting when you feel tired."

Taoism

Taoism was a major influence in making Chinese and later Japanese Buddhisms so much more positive about real life.

Taoism is a strongly pantheistic religion. Its classic scripture, the Tao te Ching, was composed some time between the sixth and third centuries BC, traditionally by Li Erh, a retired custodian of imperial archives, also known as Lao Tan or Lao Tzu.

The Tao te Ching never speaks of a transcendent God or God. Its central focus is the Tao or Way, conceived of as a mysterious and numinous unity, infinite and eternal, underlying all things and sustaining them. But there is a profound religious reverence and respect for the Tao, and an acceptance of the need for human submission to the Tao. In this sense the Tao is discussed much in the same spirit as Pantheism discusses the divinity of the Universe.

> *The Great Tao flows everywhere . . .*
> *All things depend on it for life,*
> *and it does not turn away from them.*
> *One may think of it as the mother of all beneath Heaven.*
> *We do not know its name, but we call it Tao . . .*
> *Deep and still, it seems to have existed forever.*

The ideal of Taoism was to live in harmony with the Tao and to cultivate a simple and frugal life, avoiding unnecessary action: "Being one with nature, he [the sage] is in accord with the Tao."

Lao Tzu's most famous successor, Chuang Tzu, emphasized the pantheistic content of Taoism even more strongly. "Heaven and I were created together, and all things and I are one," he said.

> *When Tung Kuo Tzu asked Chuang Tzu where the Tao was, he replied that it was in the ant, the grass, the clay tile, even in excrement: "There is nowhere where it is not . . . There is not a single thing without Tao."*

Chuang Tzu envisaged a kind of mystical union with the Tao, and a stoic acceptance of life and death: "He would follow anything, he would receive anything. To him everything was in destruction, everything was in construction. This is called tranquillity in disturbance."

Ancient Greece and Rome

There was time when it seemed that Pantheism could have achieved a similar prominence in the West as in the East. Between the third century BC and the fourth century AD three great philosophical systems vied for first rank among the educated elite. Of these, Stoicism was thoroughly pantheistic. Neo-Platonism was inclined to Pantheism, but of a more idealistic and world-rejecting type. And Pantheism was present even among the physicalist Epicureans.

Probably the first identifiable pantheists in the West were the earliest of all Greek philosophers, from the Western, Ionian shore of Asia Minor (modern Turkey). Thales of Miletus, one of the seven sages of antiquity, taught that the universe had a soul and was full of divinities. His Miletan contemporary, Anaximander, believed that all things were made from the "apeiron" or infinite substance:

> *The infinite has no beginning, . . . but seems to be the beginning of other things, and to surround all things and guide all . . . And this is the divine, for it is immortal and indestructible.*

But the clearest expression of this early Pantheism came from Heraclitus, of Ephesus, not far up the coast from Miletus. Heraclitus was a notorious misanthrope and haughtily refused to take part in the politics or religious ceremonies of his native city. The story has it said that he eventually withdrew into the mountains to live off grass and herbs.

Heraclitus' writings have survived only in fragments which are often dense and obscure. He is perhaps best known for his doctrines that fire is the basic substance of all things, and that everything is in a process of ceaseless change:

> *Eternity is a child at play, playing draughts . . . No-one can step twice into the same river, nor touch mortal substance twice in the same condition. By the speed of its change, it scatters and gathers again.*

Heraclitus mocked conventional religious belief, and held that the cosmos was its own maker and creator:

> *The Cosmos was not made by gods nor men, but always was, and is, and ever shall be, ever living fire, igniting in measures and extinguishing in measures.*

The first major movement of Pantheism in the West, Stoicism, was profoundly influenced by Heraclitus. The school was founded in the early third century BC by Zeno of Citium in Cyprus. Zeno was probably an old man when he began teaching to small groups in the Athenian market place, in a painted colonnade known as the Stoa Poikile which gave the group its name.

Today Stoicism is best known for the uncomplaining acceptance of fate and suffering which it encouraged - but it had a fully developed philosophy covering logic, ethics and physics. Stoic science was wise before its time: it taught that the sun was a huge sphere of fire, bigger than the earth, and that the moon shone with reflected light.

The Stoics believed that the Universe itself was a divine being, a living thing endowed with soul and reason. All conventional gods were merely names for different powers of the cosmic God. Everything in the earth and heavens was the actual substance of God.

The Stoics were physicalists, and yet they saw this God as a being with intelligence and purpose, a "designing fire" pervading every part of the universe. "God is the common nature of things, also the force of fate and the necessity of future events," wrote Zeno's follower Chrysippus. "In addition he is fire, and the ether . . Also things in a natural state of flux and mobility, like water, earth, air, sun, moon and stars; and he is the all-embracing whole."

In time Stoicism became one of the leading schools of thought in the classical world. It viewed itself as a philosophy, not as a religion, and so never had organized rites or churches.

Its most famous follower was Marcus Aurelius, who ruled the Roman Empire from 161 to 180 AD. Marcus seems to have led an unhappy life, much of it spent on military campaigns in Eastern Europe. His wife Faustina was notoriously unfaithful, and his wastrel son Commodus became the worst Roman emperor since Nero and Caligula. Marcus' Meditations were written from day to day, often in response to the stress of supreme power or the fear of death in battle.

Marcus saw the Universe as "one living being, having one substance and soul." All things were interconnected with a sacred bond. Nature was in a process of constant change, using the universal substance to mould now a horse, then when the horse dies a tree, then a man.

It was crucial, Marcus believed, for us to realize that we were part of the universe and to be in harmony with it:

> *Everything harmonizes with me, which is harmonious to thee, O Universe. Nothing for me is too early or too late, which is in due time for thee . . . From thee are all things, to thee all things return . . . Pass then through this little space of time conformably to nature and end your journey in content, just as an olive falls off when it is ripe, blessing nature which produced it, and thanking the tree on which it grew.*

Another leading classical strand of thought was founded by Epicurus (341-270 BC). Epicureanism was a physicalist philosophy. It taught that nothing existed except atoms and the void in which they moved. It did pay lip service to the existence of the classical gods, but described them as perfect beings living in a distant realm, with no interest in the earth and no impact on human affairs.

The Roman poet Lucretius gave the most thorough expression to Epicureanism in his poem On the Nature of Things, written in the first century BC. For Lucretius, as for the Stoics, even the spirit was made of a refined type of matter. But despite his scepticism about traditional religions, he had a deep pantheistic respect for the universe. He believed it was infinite in all directions and full of many inhabited worlds like our own.

He also had a religious love for nature, which he addresses as Venus:

> *You alone govern all things, and without you nothing emerges into the regions of light or becomes joyous and loveable . . . A divine pleasure and awe seizes me, that nature stands so clearly unveiled in every part.*

The final flower of Pantheism in the classical world was the neo-Platonist philosopher Plotinus (205-270) who lived and taught in Rome. He made an unlikely pantheist. He shunned public baths with their promiscuous nudity. "Plotinus seemed ashamed of being in a body," Porphyry, his favourite pupil, wrote in the biography of his teacher. Porphyry also wrote down all of his master's lectures and published them as The Enneads.

The time when Plotinus lived was chaotic, marked by famines, plague, wars and civil wars, and the near-collapse of the Roman empire. So perhaps it is not surprising that Plotinus was a world-rejecting type of pantheist who hoped that death would bring him into complete union with God.

He envisaged God as an impersonal Unity - infinite, eternal, with no spatial location, and even without thought, knowledge or movement. This idea is strikingly close to that of Taoism.

Plotinus imagined that the universe was made by God (or the One, as Plotinus called him) out of his own substance, by progressive emanation, somewhat like a balloon being blown up. "The One, perfect in seeking nothing, possessing nothing and needing nothing, overflows and creates a new reality by its superabundance," Plotinus taught.

The One emanated first into Intellect, a purely spiritual form, then into Soul, which in turn animated the physical world. Soul is present even in the lowest forms of existence, but these are so far removed from divinity that Plotinus sometimes calls matter evil.

> *This universe is a single living being, embracing all living beings within it, and possessing a single Soul that permeates all its parts . . . A sympathy pervades this single universe, and . . in a living and unified being there is no part so remote as not to be near, through the very nature that binds the living unity in sympathy.*

Soul enlivens all things with its whole self and all Soul is present eve-
rywhere. . . And vast and diversified though this universe is, it is one
by the power of soul and a god because of soul. The sun is also a god,
because ensouled, and the other stars, and if we ourselves partake of
the Divine, this is the cause.

Plotinus had a powerful influence on later Christian thought, and on Christian mysticism. He told Porphyry that his chief goal was to strive for mystical union with the One:

Often I have woken to myself out of the body, become detached from
all else and entered into myself; and I have seen beauty of surpassing
greatness, and have felt assured that then especially I belonged to the
higher reality, engaged in the noblest life and identified with the Di-
vine.

If Marcus Aurelius had encouraged Stoicism as the official religion of Rome, the cultural history of the following 1500 years might have turned out very differently. But the Roman emperors from Constantine on chose to favour and later enforce Christianity as the state religion, and Pantheism was forced underground. For some 1200 years, from the fourth century until the end of the sixteenth, Pantheism in the West appeared only as occasional sparks amid the great theistic religions of Judaism, Christianity and Islam.

3: The History of Pantheism: Monotheistic and modern.

The three major Western religions, Judaism, Christianity and Islam, all believe in a similar kind of God. He is a God who existed from all eternity, who created and now rules the universe. A god who has planned a vast cosmic drama that will end in the final judgement of all human souls and the winding up of the history of the earth as we know it. A God who extends far beyond space and time and is far greater than the universe.

Yet none of these religions believe in a totally distant and separate God. Even their central doctrines tend to be panentheistic (see page xx) - that is, they believe that God is active and present in some way in the universe, as well as extending beyond it.

But they also have statements that can be read in a more clearly pantheistic way. Again and again pantheists have arisen from within all three religions, sometimes disguising their views carefully enough to avoid persecution - sometimes being condemned as heretics.

Judaism: Old Testament, Talmud and Kabbalah

Yahweh, the God of the Old Testament, is often described as being totally distant and unapproachable. Yet from the time of Moses' first encounter with the burning bush on Mount Sinai, God showed himself on earth. When he proclaimed his name as "I am who I am," he was asserting Himself to be Being itself. Isaiah (6:3), Jeremiah (23:24) all proclaim that God fills the whole earth with his presence.

Perhaps the most beautiful expression of this feeling is Psalm 139:

> *Whither shall I go from thy spirit?*
> *Or whither shall I flee from thy presence?*
> *If I ascend to heaven, thou art there!*
> *If I make my bed in Sheol, thou art there!*
> *If I take the wings of the morning and dwell in the uttermost parts of*
> *the sea, even there thy hand shall lead me, and thy right hand shall*
> *hold me.*

The Talmud, the body of Jewish commentaries and legal literature, was composed between the fourth and seventh centuries AD. It took these Old Testament hints much further. The rabbis of the Talmud developed the idea of God's presence on this earth, the Shechinah. God was seen as filling the world like the human soul fills the body. "There is no place where the Shechinah is not, not even a thorn bush," one rabbi declared. "He is as near to his creatures as the ear to the mouth," said another.

The Kabbalah, a system of esoteric Jewish thought developed between the twelfth and sixteenth centuries, went even further. The Kabbalistic writers did not see God and creation as two separate and distinct things. Unifying everything was Ein Sof, the endless or infinite. This was seen as an impersonal, unnameable Being without qualities, thoughts or feelings, somewhat similar to the Tao. Ein Sof emanated, like the One of Plotinus, into successive layers, culminating in angels and finally all material things. But ultimately everything remained one, and nothing existed but the divine being.

"The divine essence is below as well as above, in heaven and earth. There is nothing else," wrote the author of the Zohar, Moses de Leon.

> *"Do not say `This is a stone and not God.' God forbid!" wrote the six-*
> *teenth century Palestinian Kabbalist Moses Cordovero. "Rather, all*
> *existence is God, and the stone is a thing pervaded by divinity."*

Islam and Sufism

Within Islam, Pantheism and strong panentheism have been expressed most frequently in Sufism, the current of thought that stresses the possibility of mystical union with Allah.

Even in the Koran it is possible to find texts that support a form of Pantheism or strong panentheism:

> *To Allah belongs the East and the West, and wheresoever you turn*
> *there is the face of Allah (Sura 2:115)*
> *We created man, We know the very whisperings within him and we*
> *are closer to him than his jugular vein. (Sura 50:16)*

In Islam, it is a sin to claim that any other divinity existed beside Allah. Moreover, Allah is totally self-sufficient and needs nothing to complete him. This rigorous monotheism led some of the Sufis to the logical conclusion that nothing at all exists except Allah. And since Allah is within each one of us, it is possible to attain mystical union with Allah.

One Sufi who paid with his life for these beliefs was Al Hallaj (858-922 AD). He wrote of Allah:

> *You are the Only One in the loneliness of Eternity, You are the Only One to witness You . . . Your being far away is damnation, without You actually stepping aside; Your presence is Your knowledge, without Your moving at all . . . Nothing is above You that casts a shadow on You, nothing below that supports You, nothing before that limits You, and nothing behind that overtakes You.*

But Al Hallaj overreached himself when he said "I am the truth" - ie "I am God." By this he meant, no doubt, that theologically God was in all of us and that he felt one with God: "You have manifested yourself so much that it seems to me that there is only You in me!" But the orthodox viewed statements like these as the deepest heresy. Al Hallaj was put on trial in Baghdad, and executed after horrific public tortures.

A very different fate attended another near-pantheist, the Spanish-born theologian Ibn Arabi (1165-1240), who became feted as one of Islam's most eminent and beloved philosophers. Ibn Arabi spent decades travelling the Muslim world before settling in Damascus.

> *The cosmos is his form [Ibn Arabi wrote]. The eye perceives naught but Him . . . Allah is essentially all things. He permeates through all beings created and originated . . . He who knows himself understands that his existence is not his own existence, but his existence is the existence of Allah . . . For He will not have anything to be other than He. Indeed, the other is He, and there is no otherness.*

Moreover, Ibn Arabi said, every one of us was a facet of God's existence:

> *The knower and that which he knows are both one, and he who unites and that with which he unites are one, and seer and seen are one . . . Thou[the reader] art not thou: thou art He. Thou never wast nor wilt be, Thou art neither ceasing to be nor still existing. Thou art He.*

Christianity

The roots of Christian Pantheism reach back to the New Testament itself. Of course, we can never be sure what Jesus himself believed, because he never wrote anything down, and what was eventually written contains a great deal of enigmatic and paradoxical material. But there are remarks in the New Testament that can be given a pantheistic interpretation.

> *When the Pharisees asked Jesus when the Kingdom of God would come, he replied: "The Kingdom of God does not come with your careful observation, nor will people say `Here it is' or `There it is', because the Kingdom of God is within you."* (Luke 17:20).

The early apocryphal Gospel of Thomas, discovered at Nag Hammadi in Egypt, has Jesus saying:

> *The Kingdom is within you, and it is outside of you . . . Cleave a piece of wood, I am there. Raise up a stone, and you will find me there.*

St Paul often claimed that the spirit of God dwelt in each one of us, and expressed a clearly pantheistic emotion when he addressed the Athenians. God made us, he said, so that we should seek him; "though he is not far from each one of us. For in Him we live and move and have our being," (Acts 17:27-28). Paul was actually quoting a Stoic poet here, with approval.

These few sayings have provided inspiration and biblical justification for pantheists and near pantheists in the Christian tradition throughout the ages, and they are especially influential today.

Most Christian mystics were panentheists rather than true pantheists: they believed not that the Universe was God, but that God was the Universe, and also greater than the Universe. He was part immanent in real things, and part transcendent, above and beyond them.

True Pantheism has rarely been recorded in Christianity, for the very good reason that until the late seventeenth century it would have been punished as profound heresy. The few pantheists who did stick their necks out often paid for it with the burning of their books and often with excommunication and death. These included two thirteenth century theologians at the University of Paris, David of Dinant and Amalric of Bena.

> *It is manifest* [wrote David], *that there is only one substance, not only of all bodies, but also of all souls, and that this substance is nothing else but God Himself. It is clear, then, that God and Matter and Mind are the same substance.*

The works of David and of Amalric were destroyed as heretical, and in 1210 nine of Amalric's followers were burned at the stake.

The Dominican theologian Meister Eckhart (1260-1327) was perhaps the most pantheistic of Christian mystics. Eckhart taught that all things were contained in God, who was the being of every being, in the innermost part of each and every thing. By transcending our selves we could become one with God in mystic union. It took a while for his contemporaries to challenge the heresy of his position. He was highly regarded for most of his life, but at the age of 66 he was formally charged with heresy, and his "errors" were condemned in a papal bull of 1329.

> *God is infinite in his simplicity and simple in his infinity [Eckhart wrote]. Therefore he is everywhere and is everywhere complete . . . Only God flows into all things, their very essences. Nothing else flows into something else. God is in the innermost part of each and every thing, only in its innermost part.*
>
> *All things are contained in the One, by virtue of the fact that it is one. for all multiplicity is one, and is one thing, and is in and through the One. . . The One is not distinct from all things. Therefore all things in the fullness of being are in the One by virtue of its indistinction and unity.*

Post-Christian Pantheism: Bruno to Toland.

By the end of the sixteenth century science was beginning to emerge, still nervously, from the Church's fetters. Classical Greek and Roman authors were translated and printed, and made accessible to a wider public. Copernicus' theory that the earth moved around the sun had demoted the earth from its status as centre of the universe.

But it was not until well after the Reformation that pantheists, atheists and other non-Christians dared to express their philosophy more openly in Europe. And in Catholic countries subject to the Inquisition it was still fraught with danger.

The first truly post-Christian pantheist in Europe, Giordano Bruno (1548-1600) paid for his intellectual courage with his life. The young Bruno became a Dominican monk, but fled Italy under suspicion the heresy and murder. He spent most of his life roaming restlessly between England, France and Germany where he could be safe from the Catholic Church's authority. He was, beyond all doubt, a heretic in the church's terms.

Like Lucretius, Bruno believed that the universe was infinite, containing an infinity of worlds just like our own. For him the Universe was God, and God was the Universe. Every individual thing had something of the whole within itself.

> *There is one simple Divinity found in all things, once fecund nature, preserving mother of the universe in so far as she diversely communicates herself, casts her light into diverse subjects, and assumes various names. . . This Nature is none other than God in things . . . Animals and plants are living effects of Nature; Whence all of God is in all things . . . Think thus, of the sun in the crocus, in the narcissus, in the heliotrope,*

in the rooster, in the lion. . . . To the extent that one communicates with Nature, so one ascends to Divinity through Nature.

In 1591 Bruno fatefully accepted a tutorial post in Venice to a young nobleman, Zuane Mocenigo. After a dispute, Mocenigo denounced Bruno to the Inquisition. Transferred to Rome, Bruno spent his last years in the Holy Office prison. On February 17, 1600, he was burned alive at the Campo dei Fiori where his statue stands today.

The most influential of all early modern pantheists was the philosopher Benedict Spinoza (1632-1677). Born into a family of Jewish refugees from Portugal, Spinoza was trained in Talmudic scholarship but soon developed an unconventional theology of his own. When this became known, he was summoned before a rabbinical court and even offered money to recant. When he refused, he was excommunicated. He earned a humble living as a lens-grinder, and died of consumption in 1677.

Spinoza's chief work, the *Ethics*, is a difficult and abstract book. Although Spinoza uses the word God very often in the phrase *deus sive natura* - God or nature - there is no mention of nature's beauty. But there is a totally uncompromising Pantheism quite close to the viewpoint of Ibn Arabi. All individual things were only different ways in which God's character was expressed:

> *Nothing exists but God . . . God is one, that is, only one substance can be granted to exist in the universe . . . Whatsoever is, is in God, and without God nothing can be, or be conceived.*

True to its title, the Ethics offers a moral code. For Spinoza the chief goal of human life is knowledge of God. This knowledge brought a kind of Buddhist or Stoical conquest of pain and suffering: knowing that everything that happens is a necessary part of God would help us to accept our lives joyously.

Throughout its long history up till the end of the seventeenth century, Pantheism never had its own characteristic name. It was known as Stoicism, or the Brunian philosophy, or Spinozism. It was not until the early eighteenth century that the words pantheist and Pantheism came into use.

The man credited with coining the word pantheist was the Irish writer John Toland (1670-1721). Toland is best known for his 1696 book *Christianity not Mysterious*, which argues that theology is perfectly understandable to reason, without the need for scriptural revelation. The book seems mild today: but it was condemned by the Grand Jury of Middlesex and burned by the public hangman in Dublin.

Toland had blighted his career and never lived this episode down. From then on he led an insecure life mainly as a hack writer of political tracts. The fall-out also taught him to keep as a careful secret the pantheistic beliefs he had probably nurtured since the early 1690s. In fact it was not until 1720, when he was living in obscure poverty with nothing more to lose, that he stated his beliefs in writing, in the *Pantheistikon*.

Toland was the first modern pantheist to combine a religious reverence for the Universe, with respect for science, and a belief that everything is made of matter. A pantheist, he wrote to the German philosopher Leibniz, was one of those persons "who believe in no other eternal being but the universe." When asked for a brief statement of his credo, Toland replied, "The sun is my father, the earth my mother, the world is my country and all men are my family."

Toland's *Pantheistikon* broke new ground in another way. It was the first call for any kind of organization for celebrating Pantheism. Toland dreamed of a network of Pantheist gentleman's clubs, whose members would meet for dinner, games and philosophical debate. Each meeting would begin with a short liturgy, including recital of a pantheist credo:

> *All things in the world are One, and One in all things. What is all in all things is God, and God is eternal, has not been created, and will never die.*

Living in an age of continued intolerance, Toland suggested that Pantheists would be wise to remain secret. The *Pantheistikon* was written in Latin, published secretively, and distributed only to a few close friends. Probably Toland never actually set up the kind of pantheist club he dreamed of, though an undocumented tradition has him as the founder of a Druid order, the Universal Bond. He died in Putney in 1721.

The pantheistic nineteenth century

The works of Bruno, Spinoza and Toland were slow in spreading at first. Spinoza's work was criticized by European philosophers of the enlightenment, and dismissed as atheism by Christians. But in the later eighteenth century Spinoza began to gain a wider following, beginning in Germany, spreading to England and from there to America.

Pantheism was the religious heart of the Romantic poets. Germany's greatest poet, Goethe (1749-1832) was strongly influenced by Bruno and Spinoza. Even as a boy of seven he worshipped nature, and built a secret altar in his room, made of minerals and other natural objects and candles. "Everything which exists," he wrote as a student, "necessarily pertains to the existence of God, because God is the one Being whose existence includes all things."

> *What kind of God would thrust only from outside,*
> *letting the cosmos circle round his finger?*
> *He likes to drive the world from inside,*
> *harbours the world in Himself, Himself in the world,*
>
> *so all that lives and weaves and is in Him*
> *never wants for his power or his spirit.*

The German idealist philosophers Schelling and Hegel (1770-1831) were pantheists. Hegel's concept of God has been very influential on later Christian theology. He saw God not as a distant creator figure or judging father. Rather God was the World Spirit, clothing himself in matter and energy. The whole of history was God's self development, embodied in heroic individuals like Napoleon and in nations like Germany. "What God creates he himself is . . . God is manifestation of his own self."

In England the greatest Romantic poets of the early nineteenth century were pantheists, at least for a time in their lives.

"God only acts and is," wrote William Blake (1757-1827) "through existing beings and men." Percy Bysshe Shelley (1792-1822) is better known as an atheist, but even in his *Essay on Atheism*, he attacks only the idea of a creator God, not the pantheistic idea of a world spirit: "There is no God. This negation must be understood solely to affect a creative Deity. The hypothesis of a pervading Spirit co-extensive with the Universe remains unshaken."

For much of his later life, Samuel Taylor Coleridge (1770-1850) accepted Trinitarian Christianity, he but dallied with Pantheism in poems like *The Aeolian Harp* and *Frost at Midnight*. In the latter he hopes that his child will wander through lakes and mountains, seeing in them:

> *The lovely shapes and sounds intelligible*
> *Of that eternal language, which thy God*
> *Utters, who from eternity doth teach*
> *Himself in all, and all things in himself.*

The best known of the English pantheistic poets was Wordsworth (1770-1850) and in his youth this tendency was strong. In the first version of the *Prelude*, written in 1799 when he was as 29, he writes of "that spirit of religious love in which I walked with Nature," a love so intense that it leaves little room for a separate God:

> *Along his infant veins are interfused*
> *The gravitation and the filial bond*
> *Of Nature, that connect him with the world.*
> *Emphatically such a being lives*
> *An inmate of this active universe . . .*
> *I felt the sentiment of being spread*
> *O'er all that moves, and all that seemeth still . . .*
> *for in all things*
> *I saw one life, and felt that it was joy.*

Pantheism's fascination for poets persisted throughout the nineteenth century. "Closer is He than breathing, and nearer than hands and feet," wrote Alfred Tennyson in *The Higher Pantheism*. "All is Thou and in Thee." Oscar Wilde's poem, *Panthea*, is strongly pantheistic.

Across the Atlantic Walt Whitman (1819-1892) America's best loved poet, and her favourite essayist, Ralph Waldo Emerson (1803-1822) were both pantheists. Whitman wrote:

I hear and behold God in every object. . .
Why should I wish to see God better than this day?
I see something of God each hour of the twenty four,
and each moment then,
In the faces of men and women I see God, and in my own face in the
glass.

Emerson's 1836 *Essay on Nature* breathes a powerful Pantheism of nature:

In the woods, we return to reason and faith. There I feel that nothing
can befall me in life - no disgrace, no calamity (leaving me my eyes),
which nature cannot repair. Standing on the bare ground - my head
bathed by the blithe air and uplifted into infinite space - all mean ego-
tism vanishes. I become a transparent eye-ball; I am nothing! I see
all; the currents of the Universal Being circulate through me; I am
part or parcel of God.

In Germany Pantheism was still going strong right up to the first World War. It surfaced in Richard Wagner's *Tristan and Isolde* (1865), which ends with Isolde's love-death merging into the divine unity:

In the cosmic spirit's
wafting unity
to drown -
to sink down -
unconscious -
highest ecstasy.

And in Gustav Mahler's *Song of the Earth* (1908):

Oh beauty, oh earth, drunk with eternal love and life.
All over, everywhere,
the blessed earth blossoms in spring
and greens again.
Everywhere and forever,
the distances shine with blue haze
Forever, forever.

The early years of the twentieth century saw the foundation of the first pantheist movement in the modern world, by the great German biologist

Ernst Haeckel (1834-1919). Haeckel's Pantheism was close to that of Toland and Lucretius. He saw God as identical with the physical universe, and believed we should relate to it through science, art and religion. His own feelings for the aesthetics of natural form was powerfully expressed in beautiful drawings of sea creatures, corals and plankton, published in his book *Art Forms in Nature.*

In 1906 Haeckel launched the Monist League to embody and spread these ideas. At its peak the League had some 6,000 members in German speaking countries. Unfortunately Haeckel added his own brutal political ideas on race and eugenics to the Monist League agenda. His love for nature and his profound respect for evolution led him to monstrous ethical conclusions, very distant from any other form of Pantheism before or since. He believed that humans should actually help evolution along in the work of natural selection, by killing unfit children and even sickly adults, to prevent them spreading their genes. He also recommended the execution of all serious criminals.

There is little doubt that Haeckel's views, and the appearance of scientific backing he gave them, influenced German racism and eugenics, and found realization in the Nazi policy of "euthanasia" for the mentally unfit. However, after they won power the Nazis did not show any favour to the Monist League. They were more interested in Nordic paganism than in Pantheism, and the League was disbanded in 1933.

Retreat in the twentieth century

Pantheist ideas were so dominant in the nineteenth century that some writers of the time saw it as the culmination of all religious development until then, and predicted the triumph of Pantheism in the following century. But the optimism was premature. Pantheism was too positive and too optimistic a faith for the first half of the disastrous twentieth century.

Nevertheless some very eminent pantheists maintained their views throughout these difficult times.

The United States' greatest architect, Frank Lloyd Wright (1867-1959), was a strong pantheist. He claimed that Nature was the source of his inspiration, and in his building he followed the principles of nature. "I believe in God," he wrote, "only I spell it Nature":

> *God is the great mysterious motivator of what we call nature, and it has been said often by philosophers, that nature is the will of God. And, I prefer to say that nature is the only body of God that we shall ever see.*

One of the greatest US poets of the twentieth century, Robinson Jeffers (1887-1962) held very similar pantheist beliefs. Jeffers' poems are steeped in nature, seen just as she is, elemental, beautiful yet often brutal. His Pantheism was very close indeed to that of John Toland, and philosophically identical with that of today's World Pantheist Movement:

> *I believe that the universe is one being, all its parts are different expressions of the same energy, and they are all in communication with each other, therefore parts of one organic whole . . . This whole is in all its parts so beautiful, and is felt by me to be so intensely in earnest, that I am compelled to love it, and to think of it as divine. It seems to me that this whole alone is worthy of the deeper sort of love; and there is peace, freedom, I might say a kind of salvation, in turning one's affections outward toward this one God, rather than inwards on one's self, or on humanity, or on human imaginations and abstractions - the world of spirits.*

The greatest English novelist of this century, D. H. Lawrence, was a pantheist. On the fly-leaf of a book about Fra Angelico, he penned a concise statement of his beliefs, which was privately published in 1935 as one of the shortest books of all time - a single paragraph:

> *This is how I "save my soul" by accomplishing a pure relationship between me and another person, me and other people . . . me and the animals, me and the trees or flowers, me and the earth, me and the skies and sun and stars, me and the moon; an infinity of pure relationships . . . that makes our eternity for each one of us . . . This, if we knew it, is our life and our eternity; the subtle, perfected relation between me and my whole circumbient [sic] universe.*

Finally, the greatest scientist of the twentieth century, Albert Einstein (1879-1955) was a pantheist. Of course Einstein is best known for his theory of relativity, but he frequently pronounced on political and ethical questions. Einstein made it plain that he did not believe in any kind of personal human-like God who would work miracles and answer prayers in defiance of the laws of nature, and reward and punish us in the afterlife.

For Einstein God was the order and harmony and law of the universe itself, and science was in that sense a religious quest.

> *I have never imputed to Nature a purpose or goal, or anything that could be understood as anthropomorphic. What I see in Nature is a magnificent structure that we can comprehend only very imperfectly, and that must fill a thinking person with a feeling of humility. This is a genuinely religious feeling that has nothing to do with mysticism.*

But people like Einstein, Lloyd Wright and Lawrence, eminent though they were, were isolated sparks in the dark years from 1914 to the 1950s.

They did not make up a self aware movement. It was not till the last decades of the twentieth century that Pantheism began to regain some of its nineteenth century promise, as we shall explore in the concluding chapter.

4. Core beliefs: Reverence of the Universe.

Two core sentiments lie at the heart of Pantheism.
- All pantheists feel that the Universe is in some sense worthy of the deepest reverence.
- And they accept that the Universe is in important senses a unified whole of which all individual things are interdependent parts.

For pantheists there is no part of "God" held in reserve, somewhere beyond the edge of time and space. The object of pantheist reverence did not precede the Universe, it does not extend outside the Universe, it is not greater than the Universe. When we use the word Universe here with a capital, we include any other universes, beyond the one we can see with our instruments, that science may one day reliably demonstrate - these would still be part of the Omniverse, the totality of everything that exists.

Why pantheists revere the Universe

As we have seen, pantheism has traditionally used some of the language of theism but in quite different ways. While a modern naturalistic pantheist would say: "I feel a deep religious reverence for the Universe and Nature," a traditional pantheist would say: "The Universe is God."

Some traditional pantheist philosophers have tried to prove that God and the Universe are identical through logical argument. Spinoza used complicated scholastic definitions to try to prove that nothing except God could possibly exist.

There are simpler proofs of the central pantheist belief using theistic terms. According to theists, before the Creation nothing existed except God.

Therefore the only thing out of which he could make creation was his own substance. By this argument the Universe would be, or would at least part of, God's substance.

Another proof starts with the theological definition, provided by St Anselm of Canterbury, that God is "that being than whom no greater can be conceived." Now if we define the Universe as the totality of everything that exists, then it is impossible to conceive of anything greater than the Universe. So the Universe itself must be Anselm's greatest being, and therefore the Universe is the true "supreme being."

More modern approaches would set out, not to prove that the Universe is the "God" mentioned in scriptures, but to show that the Universe is worthy of the deepest religious reverence, by comparing its real powers with the powers that people think God possesses.

Throughout the ages, sceptics have suggested that the supposed powers of the gods were myths, based on the real powers of nature. Zeus or Thor embodied the power of storms. Apollo symbolized the power of the sun, Neptune that of the sea, and so on.

Pantheists take this argument further and suggest that the main characteristics of the God of Judaism, Christianity and Islam are based on Nature and the Universe. The theist God, they would suggest, is a kind of personified metaphor for the Universe.

God is said to be the creator: overwhelmingly powerful, all-knowing, omnipresent, infinite and eternal. Pantheists would argue that the Universe itself possesses most of these qualities. Indeed it is indeed the only thing we know to possess these qualities, and our only source of experience of these qualities.

The Universe is our creator. We are made of star stuff. Our hydrogen and much of our helium emerged in the first few minutes after the big bang, the rest of our elements were forged by fusion inside stars, strewn across space in novae and supernovae, and transformed into heavier elements in successive star generations. Finally they were regathered in our solar system providing the elements that allowed life to evolve.

The Universe can also destroy us. In past mass extinctions, most life on earth has been wiped out through large meteor collisions or nearby supernovae, which could recur in the future. The power of nature here on earth can destroy us through earthquakes, volcanic eruptions, storms and floods, and epidemics.

So in a very real sense the Universe and Nature are, as far as we are concerned, overwhelmingly powerful.

The Universe is omnipresent because it is filled with energy spreading from every part to every other part. Radiation of various types reaches us from every corner of the universe and from the deepest reaches of time past - we are bathed in microwave radiation from the very earliest moments of the universe's existence.

The Universe is not all-knowing in the human sense. Yet every part of it is, in a sense, "aware" of every other through the exchange of photons and gravity conveying information about the state of even the most distant regions.

The universe our telescopes can detect does not appear to be infinite. What we can see today covers a diameter of no more than 20-30 billion light years. Nor is the universe as far as we know eternal - cosmologists estimate it to be between 10 and 15 billion years old. But from our tiny human perspective, these times and distances are virtually eternal and infinite.

The most prevalent modern hypothesis of cosmic origins, the inflation theory of Allan Guth and Andrei Linde, predicts that our local universe is just one of a foam of universes bubbling into existence from a dense energy field. The totality of all these universes, the greater Universe, or Multiverse, or Omniverse, would in fact be truly infinite and eternal.

The Universe as eternal, or as its own creator

Humans are naturally impelled to seek for the causes of everything. That urge explains a large part of our success as a species, and has driven us to investigate links and to develop new technologies.

This same urge has led people to seek for the cause of the whole Universe. Theists like Thomas Aquinas have argued that we see from experience that nothing exists without a cause. Since it is unacceptable for a chain of causes to be infinite, the Universe itself must have a first cause. This has been one of the main arguments for the existence of a creator God.

Sceptics have always challenged this argument. Since we have no problems imagining an infinite future, it is hard to see any overwhelming reason why the chain of causes in the past should not be infinite.

The argument for a creator God also has a very serious logical flaw. It is based on the premise that everything requires a cause - and yet theists accept that one thing does exist without a cause: God himself. This tends to undermine the basic premise of the argument. God is thought to exist without a cause. But if one thing can be self-existing, why can this one thing not be the Universe itself?

When we say something has a cause, we mean that something preceded it which brought it about - cause precedes effect. But by definition the Universe includes all time and space, and no time could have preceded it. It seems unreasonable to ask for the cause of a totality that includes all space and all time. The only answer theists provide to this argument is to modify the premise to say "Everything except the first cause requires a cause." But to sceptics this merely seems like an evasion, not an answer.

The idea of a creator God does not really answer the question of cause, but simply pushes it back one level. The question of the cause of God's own existence remains unanswered, yet theists draw a boundary here to our urge to question causes.

As the Scottish philosopher David Hume said, in a remark that suggests a close affinity with Pantheism:

> *If I am still to remain in utter ignorance of causes . . . I shall never esteem it any advantage to shove off for a moment a difficulty which . . must immediately, in its full force, recur upon me. . . . . It were better, therefore, never to look beyond the present material world. By supposing it to contain the principle of its order within itself, we really assert it to be God; and the sooner we arrive at that divinity, the better.*

But if the Universe had no external creator, then where did it come from? One possibility is that the universe "created" itself, or rather emerged spontaneously, out of virtually nothing. Several modern theories of cosmology assume that the universe began as a fluctuation in a quantum vacuum, or arose from an energy field empty of matter. However, strictly speaking a vacuum or energy field is not "nothing." One would still need to explain where the field itself came from.

An attractive possibility is that the Universe existed eternally and had no beginning. This does not appear to be true of our own local universe, but increasing numbers of physicists believe that there are multiple Universes either coexisting with our in parallel dimensions or totally separate from ours in other dimensions. The totality could be a Multiverse or Omniverse, an eternally bubbling foam of universes each with its own laws of physics.

British cosmologist Stephen Hawking has suggested that space-time might be curved back on itself like the surface of a sphere, and like a sphere it may have no beginning or end. "The universe would be completely self-contained and not affected by anything outside it," he writes in A Brief History of Time. "It would just BE . . . What place, then, for a creator?"

Evolution as the great designer

One of the most powerful arguments for the existence of God has been the argument from design: if nature has the appearance of careful design, then there must have been a designer. But pantheists do not accept the idea of a designer separate from the universe. They believe that the universe "designed itself" through evolution.

The design argument was classically put by English clergyman William Paley in 1802. Suppose, said Paley, that we found a watch lying on the ground, in perfect working order, with all its parts moulded and assembled to tell the time of day. We would immediately assume that the watch had a designer. Since nature shows evidence of very complex and beautiful design, it follows, Paley argued, that the Universe must have a maker and designer.

The Scottish sceptic philosopher David Hume had already provided a telling answer to the design argument in his *Dialogues on Natural Religion*, published in 1776. Hume showed how apparent design could arise purely by chance in a universe of countless particles in motion. Given an infinite length of time, the particles would eventually hit on every possible combination. And some of those combinations would be forms of order which, once hit upon, would perpetuate themselves for a very long time.

Two centuries later we have more knowledge and better theories to flesh out what Hume claimed. We know how gravity gathers matter together into galaxies and then into stars that begin burning. We know how solar systems can form from rotating clouds of dust. We do not know exactly how life originated, but we do have a number of plausible theories. We know that organic molecules exist even in space. We know the physics and chemistry of how DNA reproduces itself and makes the vast diversity of organisms on this planet.

The science of self-organization is showing how inanimate matter can form quite spontaneously into regular patterns. No-one imagines that a quartz crystal requires a specific designer: it is the inevitable result of the way in which the atoms that make it up behave in their environment. Piles of sand arrange themselves into mounds with very specific angles of slope, not because there is an invisible sandpile designer at work, but simply because of gravity and the shape and weight of the grains.

Above all, in the theory of evolution, we have a brilliantly successful scientific explanation of how design emerges in the most complex things: living creatures. Evolution is a wonderful mechanism for perfecting design, and like any great designer, it has both creativity and rigorous discipline. Its main sources of creativity for new variations are random mutations and sexual recombinations of genes. The disciplined weeding out of poor design is done by the environment. Organisms that are best adapted to the environment thrive better and produce more offspring. Those that are less well adapted die out.

For pantheists, evolution is a universal force that works even on non-living things. From the very first instant of our universe, every individual thing has existed in the midst of other things, and has had to adapt to the community of beings in which it finds itself. Evolution is at work even in the realms of mind and of society. Ideas, scientific theories, technologies and products are tested against each other and the most effective survive.

Was the whole universe designed so that we should evolve?

Today, the design argument takes two main forms. One is the theory of intelligent design, as presented for example by US biochemist Michael Behe. It is really just a modernized form of Paley's argument. Behe suggests that there are biological and biochemical systems that work superbly as a whole, yet would not work at all if just one of their parts were removed. It follows that these systems could not have evolved gradually step by small step, as early evolutionists believed. Hence, Behe argues, they must have been designed. However, most modern evolution theorists accept that some changes may have occurred in sudden leaps, and also that complex systems don't originate from nothing, but emerge by adapting some pre-existing organ or process in a new way.

The second approach is more sophisticated and challenging than Paley's. It is based on the idea that, if we are here to observe it, the whole universe must be structured in such a way that conscious intelligent beings could evolve. This argument is known as the Anthropic Cosmological Principle.

In its weak form the argument simply states the obvious: if the universe were not structured in that way, then there would be no-one around to observe it. The requirements for our existence place definite constraints on the range of values that certain constants can take. But in its strong form the Anthropic Cosmological Principle suggests a lot more. It claims that the universe shows sign of having been deliberately designed with the goal of creating conscious observers like us.

The principle has some arresting evidence to back it. For example, if the mass of the neutrino had been just 1/100,000,000,000,000,000,000,000,000,000,000th of one per cent heavier, gravity would have made the universe recollapse before life had time to evolve. There are many other constants which seem to be incredibly finely-tuned to make life possible.

But even the strong form of the Anthropic Cosmological Principle relates only to the conditions needed for life to emerge and persist for long enough to allow intelligence to evolve. It can't prove that conscious beings are the purpose for which the universe was designed. If this was so, it's not clear why humans have been planned to evolve on a planet that is periodically hit by large meteorites, and suffers episodes of mass volcanism, big enough to wipe out a large proportion of all species on earth

And if the universe is tuned so that consciousness can emerge and evolve, this implies that intelligent life has probably emerged on countless billions of other planets - so humans would have no special status in the design.

Those who believe the universe designed itself have several possible answers to the strong Anthropic Cosmological Principle. One is that some basic laws that we have not yet discovered require the basic physical constants to turn out the way they did and could allow of no other permutation.

Another is that things had to turn out one way or another, and our particular arrangement is no less likely than any of the others. It only seems miraculous from our human-centred viewpoint, just as a lucky spin on the roulette table might seem to the winner like the hand of destiny.

The inflation theory assumes that our universe is just one of an infinite number of universes - each one of which may have slightly different initial conditions and laws of physics. Given so many, all permutations are possible, and our own universe is just one of them. There would be many others where life was not possible. The many-universes theory of quantum mechanics also allows for universes where life did not develop.

Cosmologist Lee Smolin suggests that black holes spew matter into new dimensions, creating new universes with slightly different laws to ours. Over time a kind of evolution would operate, favouring the kind of universe that produces black holes. This just happens to be the same kind of universe that allows stars and planets to exist for long periods of time. In other words, our kind of universe is likely to be the most common.

The Universe has the emotional impact of a God or divinity.

Another modern approach to showing how the Universe can be considered as the object of deepest religious reverence is to look at the emotions it awakes in us, and compare these with the feelings that believers have towards a personal God.

In 1917 the German theologian Rudolf Otto wrote his classic work *The Idea of the Holy*. Based on comparative study of religions East and West, Otto tried to establish exactly what qualities people felt were possessed by things seen as divine - whether these were the personal creator Gods of Western religions, or impersonal things like the Tao, Brahman or Nirvana in the East.

Otto decided that above all the nature of divinity could be summed up as a *mysterium tremendum et fascinans* - an awesome yet fascinating mystery. The three key elements were mystery, awesome power, and capacity to inspire fascination or love. Pantheists believe that the Universe itself is the only entity we know of that possesses these qualities, and therefore has the highest claim to religious reverence.

Mystery is the feeling that the divinity is something wholly other, something extraordinary and incomprehensible, producing blank wonder and astonishment in us. The universe has the capacity to do this like nothing else in our experience. Earlier generations, as they gazed at the starry heavens on a clear night, could have had some sense of this, though the universe was thought of as actually very small, not much bigger than the solar system.

But the twentieth century is the first to have the privilege of knowing the vast scope of the universe, from the smallest sub-atomic particles to the furthest quasars and clusters of infant galaxies. Today we have the priceless asset of the Hubble Space Telescope which reveals exploding stars, colliding galaxies, and luminous gas clouds birthing solar systems like our own.

Although science is continually discovering more about the inner workings of all this, what it can never do is take away our astonishment that all this stupendous immensity and complexity exists. It is all so very distant from our everyday experience that it will never cease to leave people breathless with wonder and excitement. The mystery of the ultimate origins of our universe, before the Big Bang, before the first tiny fraction of a nanosecond, may well remain forever unsolved. And the most basic mystery: why does anything exist, rather than nothing? is inherently unanswerable.

The concept of matter has moved a long way since Newton thought of it as made up of hard little particles like billiard balls, moving around predictably as they bumped into each other.

Modern science has discovered that matter is far stranger and more mysterious. Its picture of reality is one that common sense cannot grasp at all however hard it tries. The theory of relativity teaches that as we approach the speed of light, time lengthens, length shortens, and mass increases.

Quantum mechanics tells us that the ultimate particles of light, photons, are for much of the time not distinct particles in one place, but act like fuzzy waves smeared out in space. And yet whenever we put up apparatus to detect them they only ever show up as particles, pin-point dots on a detector screen. They can behave both as waves and as particles, yet humans cannot imagine anything that could be both. All this is so distant from everyday experience and everyday human ways of understanding things, that quantum mechanics remains a profound mystery even to physicists working in the field. They can do the math, but they cannot gain a common sense grasp of the underlying physical processes. Nobel prize winner Richard Feynman once remarked to his students: "Do not keep saying to yourself `But how can it be like that?' because you will get into a blind alley from which nobody has yet escaped. Nobody knows how it can be like that."

If string theory manages to unite relativity and quantum mechanics, it is unlikely to reduce the mystery. String theories demand nine or ten spatial dimensions, yet humans are not built to intuitively grasp more than three. Once again, we can do the maths of multiple dimensions, but we can't visualize the physical reality.

Otto's second aspect of divinity is the dread it inspires: the sense of an overwhelming and uncontrollable power that can transfix anyone who comes near it. A power that instils a sense of its absolute superiority, and makes us feel our personal submission to it and submergence in it.

No-one has ever seen the power of the God of Judaism, Christianity and Islam, and whenever this power is written or spoken about it is described in terms of the power of nature: when this God smites people, he does so with thunderbolts, earthquakes, plagues and other natural means.

In fact pantheists believe that claims about God's awesome power are simply symbolic expressions of the awesome power of nature and the universe. No-one who has witnessed or seen films of lightning, volcanic eruptions or arching solar flares can be other than awestruck at the terrifying levels of power involved. The sun alone is so powerful that we cannot gaze at it directly even for more than a few seconds without being blinded.

Jews, Christians and Muslims see all these things as expressions of the power of God. Pantheists see them as expressions of the power of Nature herself, and recognizing that power, acknowledge that Nature should be regarded as the object of deepest religious awe.

The final quality of divinity that Otto identified is its beauty and power to fascinate and inspire love. "The believer," Otto wrote, "feels a something which captivates and transports him with a strange ravishment, rising often to the pitch of dizzying intoxication."

Here too pantheists would claim - and most non-pantheists would acknowledge - that these same feelings are inspired by the beauty of nature. A forest or a pounding ocean, scudding clouds, still pools or leaves falling on an autumn day can inspire the deepest feelings of love, peace and belonging. Wordsworth expresses these feelings intensely in his 1799 Prelude:

> *Among the hills I sate,*
> *Alone upon some jutting eminence*
> *At the first hour of morning, when the vale*
> *Lay quiet in utter solitude . . .*
> *Oft in those moments such a holy calm*
> *Did overspread my soul that I forgot*
> *The agency of sight.*

Again, images from the Hubble Space Telescope have shown us the indescribable beauty of the universe, from the radiance of whirlpool galaxies, to the diaphanous veils of glowing dust clouds, to the exotic blossoms of planetary nebulae.

What kind of a god is the pantheist "God"?

The word God brings up in most listeners' minds ideas of the particular God they have read about in the Bible or Koran or were taught about as children. Yet the God or gods of different religions differ in their characteristics.

The pantheist "God" is quite different from the God of Judaism, Christianity or Islam. The central object for pantheist reverence is the existing Universe. It is not a personal God. It is not a loving father, conscious of and caring for each one of us. It is simply the Reality of Being, just as it is. It is beyond personality, in any human sense. It cannot really love us, but it cannot hate us either.

> *God is without passions,* Spinoza wrote in his Ethics, *neither is he affected by any emotion of pleasure or pain . . . Strictly speaking, God does not love anyone . . . He who loves God cannot endeavour that God should love him in return.*

To some people this may seem like a cold unwelcoming sort of God, a hard God to love, a God possessing at bottom, as Richard Dawkins put it, "nothing but blind, pitiless indifference."

But the Universe can only be considered blind if we ever expected it to see; pitiless if we ever expected it to be capable of pity; indifferent if we ever expected it to be full of concern. Remove these human-centred expectations and the terms "blind, pitiless indifference" seem as little justified as blaming a stone for not feeling compassion. They almost anthropomorphize the Universe, and then condemn it for not being wise or compassionate.

The Universe is the context in which we have our feelings, and yet it has no feelings of its own. It has no malice. It does what it does. It exists and evolves and creates and destroys.

Think of some part of nature that you love - a particular forest, say. Do you expect the forest to love you back? Does it worry you that the forest cannot love you back? Does it make you love the forest any the less?

People who do like to think in terms of love, can think about love assessed by deeds rather than by possession of emotions, and reflect that the universe has provided us all with an indescribably beautiful home and a consciousness with which to appreciate it. True, it could wipe us out tomorrow in a hurricane or a meteor strike - as could the "loving" God of theist religion. But natural disasters are easier to accept if you do not imagine there is a personal God sending them to destroy the innocent and the guilty alike, or creating a world in which such things can happen. Nature does not plan or act out of anger or retribution: if a natural catastrophe strikes, it is simply the working out of the laws of nature on the social and physical structures of humankind.

The focus of pantheist reverence is not a good God. The Universe is neither good nor evil. The human categories of good and evil do not apply. It simply is. Again, this conception is easier to square with reality than the idea of an omnipotent and perfectly good God who allows or even causes devastating hurricanes, floods, epidemics claiming millions of lives - actions that in human terms would usually be seen as monstrously evil. The question why God would allow pain and evil to exist is one of the most difficult of all for theists to answer. Pantheists do not have to answer it. The Universe is what it is.

The focus of pantheist reverence is not a judging God. The Universe will not assess each one of us at the end of our lives, and assign each of us to everlasting bliss or agony. It is not sitting on our shoulder listening to all our thoughts, marking them down in our account book to be held for or against us after our death.

For many pantheists, even conscientious pantheists who strive to do good in their lives, the freedom from a judging God inside your brain is a liberating experience. There is no need to be self-conscious all the time, no need to worry about how your every thought might be assessed by a vigilant listener who has the power to punish you for all eternity.

The focus of pantheist reverence is not, in the normal human sense of the word, conscious. Some pantheists, such as the Stoics or Hegel and many modern pagans, have believed that the universe does have some kind of collective mind or soul and sense of purpose.

Naturalistic or Scientific Pantheism, however, does not believe there is anything resembling a soul or spirit to the universe. Conscious awareness emerges only after a long process of evolution, and requires at least a sensory system and a central nervous system. In the Universe there are no galactic neurones, no stellar databanks thinking collective thoughts. However, we humans are part of the Universe, and we are conscious and aware of the universe. So in this sense the Universe has consciousness within it.

The focus of pantheist reverence has a number of character traits that are quite different from the God of Judaism, Christianity and Islam. It is in a state of permanent change and motion, at every level from the restless flitting of electrons and the light-speed motion of photons, to the slow-motion drifting of tectonic plates, to the rotation of galaxies over aeons. Everything is in a state of flux, a flux that can at times be creative, and at times destructive. The destruction is an essential part of the creation. The elements for life were made available only by stars blowing off part of their substance as supernovae. The rise of the mammals was made possible only by the extinction of the dinosaurs.

And yet underlying this dynamism is a kind of peace and continuity, the continuity of a flowing stream or an ocean broken by waves. "It rests in change," Heraclitus wrote.

The pantheist concept of unity.

So far I have been referring to the focus of pantheist reverence as an "It". But in fact all individual things are part of it. We are not set over against it in distinction from it. We all have a share in it. This is what modern pagans mean when they say: "Thou art God." Not that each one of us is a separate little god in our own right, with supernatural powers and demanding to be worshipped, but that we are all part of the same universal divinity.

We are not insignificant. Each one of us is just as much part of the totality as a venerable old tree or a bright star. The pantheist "God" is the community of all beings. It is not a He, or a She, or an It. It is a "We," and a we in the broadest and most inclusive sense, embracing everything from rocks and algae, through butterflies and humans, to suns and planets.

The major Western religions are all monotheistic. They all insist on the unity of God (though in the Christian case this unity has also to accommodate the Trinity). Pantheists too are in a sense monotheistic.

Their one focus of reverence is the universe, and they have a profound belief in the unity of all things in nature and the universe. Indeed the pantheist belief in unity is stronger that the theistic one. Theists believe that God and the Universe are at least in part separate and distinct things. For pantheists there is only one all-embracing Reality: the Universe.

Some pantheists have simply asserted this unity. Others like Spinoza have tried to prove it logically. But the unity of the universe and nature is not just a feeling or an abstract belief: it has a solid basis in science.

Everything in our universe shares a common origin. The standard big bang cosmology holds that the whole universe originated as a microscopic bubble many times less than one hundredth of a millimetre across. Thus everything that makes up the universe of today was once in the most intimate contact. As Italian novelist Italo Calvino wrote in his comic short story *All at One Point*: "Every point of each of us coincided with every point of each of the others."

Unity is not just based on a shared history. It continues throughout the present. Every single particle, every star, every being in the universe is linked by the force of gravity. A quasar on the edge of the observable universe has some effect, however small, on each of our bodies.

The whole universe is a tightly woven mesh of electromagnetic radiation. Everything emits photons of energy which race in all directions. Everything is made of the same sub-atomic constituents, held together by the same forces. And everything transmutes into everything else. The day before yesterday we were atoms in the heart of a burning star - yesterday we were dust in a collapsing proto-star - today we are living humans - tomorrow we may be soil, beetles, grass, trees, birds.

Some idealist pantheists, like Parmenides of Elea, or the authors of the Upanishads, have taken the idea of unity to extremes, and suggest that nothing really exists except the divine unity. All the everyday things we see around us, they suggest, are really just illusions.

Most modern pantheists are realists. They accept that individual things - tables, cats, moons and so on - exist independently of our minds. Although nothing is exactly the same even from one moment to the next, individual things do have a temporary existence, which can be very long in human terms.

Such is the creativity of matter that every single thing is different from every other. No two people are the same, no two snowflakes are alike, no two pebbles on the beach are identical. Without individuality, the universal unity would be utterly drab and could have no more beauty that an empty room.

Yet all these individual things are part of the same Universe, just as, on the ocean, every wave is different and partly separate, yet every wave remains part of the same ocean.

The place of humans in the universe

People who object to Pantheism are often concerned that it seems to give human an insignificant role in the cosmos. Pantheists freely accept that we are physically tiny in the scale of the cosmos, as indeed everyone must accept. Far gone are the days when we believed the earth to be the centre of the universe. Our sun is just one of over 100 billion stars in the Milky Way galaxy, which in turn is just one of perhaps 30 billion galaxies in the visible universe.

However, this does not mean that we are insignificant. We are no more and no less insignificant than anything else in the universe. Every individual thing from a mouse to a mammoth or even a star is dwarfed by the immensity of the whole - but the whole is made up of its parts.

We humans are not made insignificant by the size of the universe, any more than each of us is made insignificant by the size of the earth or the size of the world population.

We are, with our brains and our societies and technologies, the most complex beings we know of so far. We are conscious observers of the universe. Even if the universe as a whole possesses no consciousness, we do. In this sense we can be said to be a part of the consciousness of the universe, or of its self-consciousness.

And although our lives have no external purpose, we can give them the noble purpose of observing and understanding and loving the universe and nature, and of preserving nature on our planet, and of creating societies where all humans can have dignity and the opportunity for fulfilment.

Most pantheists see such a self-chosen purpose as far preferable to the purpose the God of the major Western religions assigns to humans. Even though, in Judaism and Christianity, humans are seen as central to the entire creation, their role is not a distinguished one. Since God is seen as perfect and self-sufficient, it is not at all clear why God needed to create humans, or what purpose they serve to Him.

Our role on earth seems to be simply to undergo testing, to see if we are worthy of heaven or hell: to prove to God that we obey his commands and that we believe in him and worship him. If we fail in one short lifetime we will be punished for all of eternity. And the role of the earth, indeed of the whole vast cosmos, is simply to serve as the backdrop for this brief and tiny drama.

Unity means that union is possible

If all things are, in a fundamental sense, one, then we humans are not distinct from other things in the universe. We are not superior or set apart. We share a common origin, a common history, a common substance with everything else in nature and the universe. Our very atoms are recycled continually with our surroundings. Every single breath we take unites us with everything else on earth.

Of course we often imagine that we are separate. We can feel isolated, alone, threatened or anxious in the face of nature and the universe.

But with only a small effort of thought, we can realize that our isolation is only partial. Our deepest selves can never be separated from the divine unity. We are never alone, every one of us shares in the unity. We are all part of the unity at all times. It is with us and we with it, inseparably, forever.

The realization of unity, the achievement of union, is the basis for pantheist meditation and mysticism which we shall examine in chapter seven.

5. Core Beliefs: Sacred Nature

Deep reverence for nature is the second central strand of Pantheism. If the whole universe may be seen as the central object of reverence, nature is to us its most precious and most beloved expression and the one that is most important to us in practical and ethical terms.

Pantheists believe that Nature is our mother, our security, our peace, our paradise, our past and our future. Nature made each one of us. As long as we live we remain part of nature and at our death each one of us will be reabsorbed into nature.

These beliefs have an ancient pedigree within Pantheism. Lao Tzu taught that we should live in harmony with nature, live frugally and avoid overconsumption. The Stoics taught the same. "The chief good is life according to Nature," wrote the school's founder, Zeno of Citium.

"Nature," wrote Giordano Bruno, "is none other than God in things." Spinoza usually referred to God as *deus sive natura* - God or nature.

Ultimately the pantheist reverence for nature goes even further back, to the earliest stages of our existence as a species, and may be rooted in our very genes.

Hunter-gatherer religion: humans as part of nature

Our attitude to nature has wavered during our history as a species, from reverence, to dominance and back to reverence again according to the stages of our ecological relationship with nature.

We began our career as hunter-gatherers, living by collecting wild plants and roots, hunting and fishing. As yet we did not have the numbers, nor the technologies, to destroy or to transform nature, and so we lived as an integral part of nature, learning to make the most of what nature freely offered.

Hunter-gatherer societies have a deep religious respect for all natural things. Usually their religion is animist - they believe that every animal, every tree, sometimes every rock and stream, has its own spirit or divinity. Before killing an animal or felling a tree, they often ask its permission or forgiveness.

Native Americans are the best known animists. Most tribes regard the land as their sacred mother, and all creatures as their brothers and sisters. "Every part of this soil is sacred in the estimation of my people," said Chief Seattle of the Squamish tribe, in his lament on the passing of the Indian way of life. Chief Luther Standing Bear of the Lakota wrote that kinship with all creatures of the earth, water and sky was an active principle for every Indian.

"Every seed is awakened and so is all animal life," said Sitting Bull of the Hunkpapa Teton Sioux. "It is through this mysterious power that we too have our being, and we therefore yield to our neighbours, even our animal neighbours, the same right as ourselves to inhabit this land." Black Elk, of the Oglala Sioux, wrote:

> *Every dawn as it comes is a holy event, and every day is holy, for the light comes from your Father Wakan-Tanka; and also you must remember that the two-leggeds and all the other peoples who stand upon the earth are sacred and should be treated as such. All the fruits of the wingeds, the two-leggeds and the four-leggeds are sacred and should be treated as such.*

The Indians were amazed and horrified by the way European settlers saw nature as a wilderness to be cleared and a resource to be ruthlessly plundered.

> *Forests were mown down,* Luther Standing Bear complained, *the buffalo exterminated, the beaver driven to extinction . . . The white man has come to be the symbol of extinction for all things natural in this continent*

Whereas Indians held the land in common and could not own or sell it, the whites, said Sitting Bull, "claim this mother of ours, the earth, for their own, and fence their neighbours away."

In felling, ploughing, and mining nature, the white man was simply doing what his parents and ancestors had done in Europe for countless generations. Behind their practice lay a set of religious beliefs quite different from the hunter-gatherers, which excused and justified their actions.

Agrarian religion: humans as master of nature

Gradually human populations increased, and in some places - the Near East, China, parts of the Andes and Central America - they grew too dense to be fed by hunting and gathering. At this point humans began deliberate agriculture, planting and cultivating seeds, domesticating and herding animals.

This shift changed our whole way of life, our society and our way of looking at the earth. Nature was no longer beyond our power, it was within our control and so it lost its mystery for us. Wilderness was no longer seen as our home, our shelter, our wardrobe and our larder - it became a dangerous refuge of savage beasts that preyed on livestock, a source of weeds that invaded the fields. Nature became something to be tamed and conquered rather than worshipped and placated.

Religious views changed too. The divinities of individual animals and trees vanished, and were replaced by more general gods of forces important to agriculture - sun, rain, soil, fertility. Further changes came as agrarian societies grew and states developed. Dominant gods began to emerge over the pantheon of gods - Ra, Zeus, Jupiter - resembling kings and emperors in their power.

The Israelite God Yahweh gave clear sanction to human mastery over nature: "Let us make man in our image, and let them rule over . . . the fish of the sea and the birds of the air, over the livestock, over all the earth." (Genesis 1:26). "Be fruitful and increase in number," God told Adam and Eve. "Fill the earth and subdue it." (Genesis 1:28).

The age of empires brought changes too in our views of the afterlife. Most agrarian societies around the Mediterranean originally believed that life after death was a miserable, dusty, ghostly affair, very much to be feared and avoided. But as states clashed with neighbours, wars became endemic and ordinary life was often scarred by deep anxiety, insecurity and loss of dear ones.

Gradually in Egypt, Greece, Israel and then Rome, the idea arose and spread that there was a life after death far better than life on earth. This belief in heaven radically altered people's attitudes to their real lives in their real bodies on this real earth. The body came to be seen as a mere receptacle for the much more important soul.

This earth came to be seen as merely a temporary stage for a drama that would soon be over. Loving it and looking after it was not at all important. Looking after one's eternal soul took priority.

In Judaism, Christianity and Islam, apocalyptic prophecies further diminished the value attached to this present earth. All three religions expected that sooner or later, in the end times of the Last Judgement, God himself would destroy this earth violently, only to replace it with a better one.

The age of city and industry: moving towards a new reverence for nature

These negative attitudes towards nature began to change during the industrial revolution. As cities grew, new urban classes, no longer dependent on the land for a living, came to appreciate landscape and seaside for their own sake. Geometrical gardens were ploughed under and remodelled after nature's informality. Landscape painting became popular, in which humans - if present at all - were incidental rather than central. Poets and philosophers began to write ecstatically about nature.

Today these attitudes have strengthened and spread as nature has come under new threats. Everyone over the age of twenty can remember birds they used to see in their youth, and see no more. Rainforests are being felled at the rate of 15 million hectares every year - an area three times the size of Denmark. The oceans are polluted and overfished, corals reefs are dying in every region of the globe. The earth's protective ozone layer is weakened, and global warming could bring rising seas and rapid climate change. All these human-induced changes threaten us and every other species on earth. Today we are living through the greatest mass extinction of species since the end of the dinosaurs.

Under these new circumstances, the old Biblical and agrarian attitude of human mastery over nature is no longer helpful. Even those religions that have not so far placed great value on nature are now coming to see humans not as masters but as stewards of this earth, with a responsibility to be kind to animals and to conserve nature.

Pantheism goes further than this, and sees us as members of the natural community, with a duty to behave as responsible members, and to offer restitution for the damage we have done.

Our unity with nature

Just as Pantheism sees the universe as a unity, it sees all nature on earth as a complex interacting whole. This unity is not just a belief or a warm feeling inside: it is scientific fact.

All living creatures on earth are branches of a single tree. The higher apes are our brothers and sisters in this extended family - we share over 98 per cent of our DNA with chimpanzees. But even the lowest bacterium is a distant cousin, sharing some of our genes inherited from the first living cells. All life on earth shares a common origin, whether it all started in some warm little pond, as Charles Darwin imagined; in underwater volcanic vents; or from building blocks brought in on comets or dust from space.

Our unity with nature is not just a matter of history, but a present reality that is continually renewed. Species do not exist in isolation. They live in communities, in ecosystems. Every species evolved in relation to every other part of its ecosystem. Each has its own special niche or way of life, at least a little different from every other to give all a better chance of survival. Many species have evolved in relation to their prey or predators, as well as to their competitors. Many have come to depend on each other - for pollination, seed dispersal, protection and many other mutual services.

Every habitat from a pine forest to a pond is a community, with complex cycles in which different life-forms play their role. Plants create material from light, water, air and soil. Herbivores eat plants. Carnivores eat herbivores. Finally, detritivores live by breaking down dead matter or excreta left by the others and turning it into soil or fertilizer. All the members of one habitat make up a community. They share the same home, they depend on each other in life and in death.

Gaia unites all life and non-life on the planet

This interdependence of living things extends right up to the global level. Modern geology reveals our planet to be an awesome dynamic phenomenon. Huge continental plates slowly shift as convection currents in the earth's mantle carry them along. These massive movements, coupled with vast upwellings of molten magma from close to the earth's core, have shaped the course of life's evolution.

All living things on earth are linked together with the oceans, the atmosphere, and even the rocks. Plants and algae are the planet's farms and lungs, producing basic foods and oxygen. Animals breathe in oxygen, helping to prevent this flammable gas from building up to dangerous levels where fires might start, and they provide enough carbon dioxide to keep the planet warm. Carbon, nitrogen, oxygen and water circulate in complicated cycles through living forms, rivers and seas, atmosphere and the earth's crust.

Life and planet earth are not two separable things, like a carpet lying on a floor. They have moulded each other into a unity. Life has changed the earth's atmosphere radically. Without life this would resemble the atmosphere of Mars or Venus, some 95-96 per cent carbon dioxide, 3 per cent nitrogen, and hardly any oxygen. The present composition of our atmosphere is 78 per cent nitrogen, 21 per cent oxygen, and 0.04 per cent carbon dioxide. It is only life on earth that maintains this fragile mixture: without life all the oxygen would combine with other elements.

Life has even changed the geology of the earth's crust over the aeons. Oxygen produced by ancient cyanobacteria combined with iron dissolved in the oceans, to produce insoluble iron oxides which sank forming massive layers of ironstone. The remains of ancient plants decayed to form coal and oil. The bones and shells of countless trillions of sea-animals rained to the sea bed and were compressed to create limestone and chalk.

Life has an uncanny ability to keep earth comfortable for life. Oxygen produced by the first plants created the ozone layer, filtering out harmful solar radiation and making life on land possible. Carbon dioxide breathed out by animals and methane produced by anaerobic bacteria helped to warm the earth up.

British scientist James Lovelock has proposed that the whole system of living creatures, rocks, oceans and atmosphere, combined with the process of evolution, have been able to keep global climate and atmosphere at levels broadly suitable for life over very long periods, even though the sun's output of heat has varied over time.

Lovelock's name for this self-regulating system is Gaia. Gaia or Ge is the Greek name for the goddess of the earth. For many pagans and pantheists Gaia has become almost a deity. Some think of her is a sort of super-organism with soul and awareness and purpose. But many pantheists would argue that Gaia is none other than the natural community of all life and non-life on earth - once again, a "we" rather than a "she" or and "it."

We do not need to assume that Gaia has a mind. Natural processes of evolution are enough to produce the balances that Lovelock has documented. When living things and processes produce an excess of some element, those living things that use that element multiply more rapidly and reduce its concentration. Gaia is a community that regulates itself by entirely natural mechanisms.

The human place in nature.

Belief in the unity of nature and of our living earth has important religious consequences for pantheists. It involves a return to the spiritual view of nature held by hunter-gatherers, but divested of its supernatural elements.

For pantheists, pagans, and deep ecologists, nature is more than just our hotel or our meal ticket. It is not just something we need to look after for our own self-interest. Nature is sacred. The word sacred does not mean supernatural or spooky: it refers to something we choose to imbue with profound value, and treat with the deepest respect. When God called out to Moses from the burning bush, he said: "Take off your sandals, for the place where you are standing is holy ground." But for pantheists all natural areas are sacred ground. All natural things are sacred objects which must be treated with the highest consideration and compassion.

The pantheist view of our place in nature is quite different from that of other Western religions. It does not see humans as masters of nature. Rather for the past ten thousand years we have been the scourge of nature. Our attempts to conquer and subdue have led to the impoverishment of the natural framework that ultimately supports us. We have done disastrous damage to all other species, to their habitats, and to Gaia, and it is now rebounding on us with a vengeance.

Nor does Pantheism see us as the stewards of nature. Being a steward implies managing a property for the absent master, God, but Pantheism does not believe in this absent master.

Rather Pantheism sees us as members of the natural community of all life on earth, with the same rights as other members, but with greater duties because of our greater power to do harm. We must be partners and participants in nature. This means we must live sustainably from her surplus, not dig into her capital. We must work with nature and not against her. We must promote her vast diversity, not diminish it. We will examine the ethical implications of these attitudes in more detail in the next chapter.

Our love and affinity for nature

Our love for nature is another aspect of our unity with nature. To a large extent it is a natural and physical love. We spent over 95% of our evolutionary history as a separate species in the midst of nature and as a part of nature. It is not surprising that we are instinctively attracted to the kind of environment where we evolved.

American naturalist E. O. Wilson calls this instinctive feeling "biophilia," which he defines as "the innately emotional affiliation of human beings to other living organisms." This love of nature, Wilson suggests, gave us an evolutionary advantage in the past, and could help to motivate us to defend nature today.

Whenever humans are separated from nature - in cities, or blocks of offices or flats - they try to recreate some part of nature close to them. They make gardens. They plant trees. They grow houseplants. They create bodies of moving and still water. And of course they keep pets, which are often loved as part of the family and mourned almost as strongly as humans when they die. The human love of and compassion for animals can be extraordinarily powerful.

The love of nature is not merely an abstract love. It is very often deeply rooted and attached to particular places and things: a special glade, a stretch of river, a favourite copse, a venerable tree.

We also have a deep fascination for natural form: the shape of leaves, the textures of rock, the pattern of waves, the symmetry of snowflakes. Again and again, at many different scales and in many different contexts, nature uses certain basic schemes - spiral, sphere, branching, honeycomb, radial - that we find inherently attractive.

The mathematics of nature and of human aesthetics are profoundly linked. Since Pythagoras we have known that pleasing musical harmonies are made up of simple number relationships between the wavelength of sounds. Natural ratios also play a role in the visual arts. Painters and architects from the classical world to the Renaissance have been attracted by the golden section - a division of a line into two so that the smaller segment is to the larger as the larger is to the whole line. Numerically this golden ratio is 1:1.618.

The golden ratio is not just a concept: it crops up frequently in nature. Spirals such as nautilus shells or sunflower seedheads often follow a sequence in which each section or angle is the sum of the previous two. This produces the number sequence: 1, 1, 2, 3, 5, 8, 13, 21, 34, and so on. This is known as the Fibonacci sequence, after the thirteenth century Italian mathematician who discovered it while working out how many rabbits a single pair could grow to within a year.

Remarkably, as you reach higher numbers in the Fibonacci sequence, the ratio between a number and the one after it approaches 1:1.618 - the golden ratio beloved of artists.

Nature as therapy: expanding the boundaries of the self

Nature also has the power to heal us. Most medicines are derived, directly or indirectly, from plants. But nature can heal us mentally, too. Scientific studies have shown that natural scenes can reduce stress and anxiety, and have a strong calming and restoring effect. In one experiment, patients recovering from surgery were divided into two groups. One group were put in rooms that overlooked a copse of trees, the others had a view of a plain brick wall. Those with the natural view recovered faster, had fewer complications, and needed fewer painkillers.

Nature therapist Michael Cohen tells the story of a training session for community leaders which was tense, hurried and argumentative - until a wild bird flew into the meeting room. All debate halted as everyone cooperated to help it find its way out. The bird had a strong unifying and calmative effect. Cohen has built a system of "nature therapy" to treat stress and other psychological problems. The system uses intimate contact with nature, developing our many senses to perceive nature, to reconnect with nature and find peace and balance.

The new discipline of ecopsychology sets out to understand how our alienation from nature in modern society can lead to many psychological ills. One of ecopsychology's leading figures, Theodore Roszak, theorizes that we may have an "ecological unconscious" built into us as natural physical beings, linking us to our evolutionary roots in the natural realm.

The goal of ecopsychology therapy is to re-establish healthy links between our egos and our wider ecological unconscious. It involves extending the boundaries of what we conceive as our self, linking the individual with the ecosystem, the personal with the planetary.

People exist in nature, but nature exists in people, too. As a 1990 gathering of psychologists at Harvard put it: "If the self is expanded to include the natural world, behaviour leading to the destruction of this world will be experienced as self-destruction."

Earth : the pantheist paradise

Pantheists do not believe in any separate paradise, heaven, hell or nirvana beyond this earth. They do not believe that the human soul will fly at death to some eternal realm.

Whether they believe in natural death and rejoining nature's cycles, or in reincarnation, they know that there is only one home they will ever have. This earth is our only home. This is where we are born, live and die. This is where we belong.

This earth is the only place where we can find or make our paradise. It is not some temporary launch pad toward heaven or a temporary stop-gap until God violently destroys it and replaces it with a new heaven and a new earth. This earth is indescribably beautiful, endlessly diverse, a clouded blue sapphire hanging in the deep black of space. Why should we need a new earth?

But this paradise is fragile: we are well advanced in the process of destroying its natural beauty and diversity, reducing it to drab uniformity. Earth can remain our paradise only if we take care of nature , for our children and grandchildren, but also for ourselves and for the sake of all the other species for which earth is also home.

6. Pantheist ethics: responsibilities, rights and liberties.

The systems of ethics that different religions offer have much in common. Most of it derives from common sense - rules against theft or murder, or injunctions to be charitable, for example.

But religions differ a lot in the fundamental basis of their ethics - the reasons they give for obeying the rules. In the major Western religions, moral standards claim to be based on divine commands, revealed by God by way of special messengers - Moses, Jesus, Mohammed. These commands are backed up by promises and threats of divine rewards or punishments. They focus overwhelmingly on religious and social duties, and only very marginally on environmental duties.

Eastern religions, especially in their purest philosophical forms, are very different. Their ethics are not presented as revelations by the gods, but as the conclusions of wise men like Buddha or Lao Tzu, perhaps with special wisdom, or special insights into ultimate reality.

The Eastern religions don't usually threaten supernatural rewards or punishments for obeying or disobeying their codes. Those that believe in reincarnation promise an earned progression up the scale of beings, culminating in release from suffering or union with the divine totality. They do stress social and religious obligations, but often they place great emphasis on our duties towards other living creatures.

In most of these respects Pantheism is far more like Eastern religions than Western. It makes no claim of revelation, but instead bases its ethics on its beliefs about nature and the Universe. Like Humanism, Pantheism sees human beings in their natural and social setting as the only source of human moral codes. It is our privilege, and our responsibility, to decide our ethics for ourselves.

Pantheism has no concept of a personal, judging God, and promises no supernatural rewards or punishments for good behaviour. It has no concept of sin against God, and more generally no concept of radical evil inspired by supernatural powers of darkness. And it stresses our duties to nature no less than our duties to other humans.

Critiques of pantheist ethics

Critics of Pantheism, atheism and Humanism suggest that without the threat of God's judgement hanging over them, people will ignore moral codes and commit as many crimes as they can get away with. But social reality doesn't back this up. Many non-theistic Buddhist or Taoist societies are more law-abiding than many God-fearing Christian ones - rates of crime and violence in Japan or Korea are very much lower than in Christian United States or Latin America. One can also argue that the promise of God's forgiveness if we re-pent allows people to sin now, knowing that as long as we feel sorry later God will pardon us.

The real backing for human ethics is human society and human psychol-ogy. Most children are reared to have regard for other people, and develop a conscience that makes them keep on considering others in later life. For the minority who do not, societies have systems of criminal justice that keep rea-sonable order, except in rare cases where government has completely broken down.

Pantheism is often accused of not believing in free will. It is true that some influential pantheists, like Spinoza or Einstein, rejected the idea of free will. In Spinoza's case it was because of a belief that God is infinitely perfect. Everything that happens could not happen otherwise, because all things and all events are a part of God, and so must be absolutely necessary. Einstein did not believe in free will because he thought that causality ruled supreme, with-out exception.

Critics argue that if we don't believe in free will, we may feel that we cannot control whether we act morally or not. Murderers and rapists may be-lieve that they are driven inescapably to commit the crimes they do, and might feel no restraint or guilt about it.

But nothing in the core beliefs of Pantheism says that pantheists must be determinists. Pantheism in general holds simply that the Universe is the only thing worthy of the deepest religious reverence. It does not say whether it is determined in advance - or undetermined.

Modern science points to the view that it may well be undetermined. Quantum physics suggests that even sub-atomic particles can behave in ran-dom and completely unpredictable ways. The study of chaos has shown that very small changes can magnify into enormous differences at large scale lev-els: a cricket rubbing its legs in China could cause a hurricane in Bangladesh.

It is possible then for a minute and unpredictable subatomic fluctuation to lead to massive changes at global level. Modern cosmology believes that such fluctuations in the new-born universe, just after the Big Bang, led to the way galaxies are distributed in the universe today.

There is a more serious criticism. If Pantheism believes that the universe as a whole is worthy of the deepest reverence, would this not mean that every part of the universe must be revered - even destructive parts like nuclear weapons, factory smokestacks, or mass murderers? If so, then how could we condemn crime or evil?

It's true that some extreme pantheists have taken this view, and have enacted it. The Brethren of the Free Spirit, a popular religious movement in Western Europe in the fourteenth century, believed that each one of them had become God. They could therefore commit whatever crimes they pleased with impunity, including fornication, theft and even murder.

Such movements have been rare, and their views are not supported by basic pantheist beliefs. Pantheism believes that the Universe as a whole is worthy of profound religious reverence, but this does not mean that every individual part of the universe is equally worthy. It doesn't mean that oil slicks or bits of chewing gum stuck to the pavement are to be considered sacred. Such criticisms make the simple mistake of assuming that the parts must have the same qualities as the whole - but this, of course, is not true. For example, a big oak tree may be massive and ancient, but its individual leaves are not.

Contrary to all the critics' fears, most pantheists have had noble ethical systems - even those that disbelieved in free will. The Stoics favoured a life of resignation to destiny, avoiding extreme passions. Spinoza led a model life, generous and frugal, and his chief work was called Ethics. Einstein was a pacifist dedicated to non-violence.

The human basis of all ethics

Like Humanism, Pantheism accepts that human ethics are the creation of human beings, not of supernatural gods. Humans succeeded as a species by being capable of cooperation and altruism. Unselfishness and consideration for others are a part of our basic human nature and they are very prominent in hunter-gatherer societies, where food and other survival goods are always shared generously.

As societies grew more complex, more and more rules were needed - but these were all human inventions, not divine commands.

Human standards of ethics have not stood still since the Torah/Pentateuch or the Koran - they have evolved continually. Once it was fair game to rape or kill anyone who didn't belong to your immediate tribe. Even Aristotle and St Paul defended slavery and the subordination of women. But gradually the belief that one should love and care for others has been extended to wider and wider groups of people until, today, more and more people consider the whole human race to be one family for ethical purposes.

We are currently living through another great leap forward in human ethical standards, extending rights and consideration beyond the human sphere, to animals, plants and even ecosystems.

The core of pantheist ethics: compassion for all living things.

Pantheism provides a stronger foundation for human and animal rights than most other religions. In Pantheism, the Universe as a whole is regarded as the principle focus of religious reverence. It is seen as a unity and all things are part of the unity. This means that every natural thing is an integral member of the focus of reverence: every natural thing is one spark that goes to make up the whole fire. If we revere the fire, we are obliged to respect and cherish the sparks that make it up.

Obviously, humans are more complex than most other organisms, more capable of more different types of purposive action. But as far as our *fundamental* relation to the Universe is concerned, humans are not superior to animals, nor animals to plants, nor plants to rocks or clouds or streams. All natural things are on the same level. We are all parts of a single whole, a vast community of Being.

Pantheism involves equality of respect for all natural things. However, ethics are concerned with what philosophers call "moral considerands" - that is, beings who have interests that need to be considered before taking an action. Traditionally, Western ethics were concerned primarily with ethics towards other humans, but this has been considerably broadened in modern times to cover ethics towards nature.

Of course, not all natural things require moral consideration. Non-living things like rocks cannot really be said to have interests. A volcano does not suffer if it explodes. A pebble does not get hurt or feel bad if you throw it into the sea or take it home and put it on your shelf, though the creatures living under it might need to look for a new home.

But all living things have interests, built into their genes. They all have an interest in surviving and reproducing.

Most modern ethicists drawn the moral boundary at creatures with nervous systems that have the ability to feel and experience attraction or repulsion, and, setting the barrier a little higher, perhaps also central nervous systems capable of feeling pain or pleasure. As the great eighteenth century British philosopher Jeremy Bentham put it: "The question is not, Can they reason? nor, Can they Talk? but, Can they suffer?"

Many pantheists believe that even plants have rights. True, they may have no central nervous system capable of thought, and no consciousness of suffering and pain. But scientific research does confirm that chemical processes in plants give them the equivalent of sight, smell, touch, taste and even hearing. And they do have an interest in survival and reproduction.

So for pantheists the main beings to be taken into account ethically are other humans, and other living things. Respecting these beings as equal participants in the whole means recognizing each being as a value in itself, regardless of its value to us individually, or to us as a species. Of course, it is still we humans who choose to recognize that "value in itself" in our actions, or to ignore it.

Each being is an end *in* itself, not just a means to our human ends. Each being is also an end *to* itself. It has certain goals. Respecting it as an end in itself means respecting it also as an end to itself: recognizing its goals as well as our own in all our dealings with it.

Respecting animal rights

These principles dictate that we should regard all life-forms with the deepest respect and compassion. They were not put here for us to use or abuse. They evolved in their own right, and they exist for their own benefit.

Applied to animals, these principles mean that we must try to avoid imposing pain or distress on animals. We must try as far as possible to allow them to fulfil their natural needs and to express their natural instincts.

Many pantheists take these ideas to their final conclusion and become vegetarians, avoiding all meat, or even vegans, avoiding all dairy products. However, others argue that our nearest relatives, chimpanzees, and most aboriginal human societies, hunt and eat animals, so it cannot be unnatural for humans to do so.

Humans also have rights, of course, and sometimes those rights conflict with those of other species, just as they do in the case of predator and prey, herbivore and herb, or parasite and host. As a minimum we need food, shelter, and clothing. It can be argued that to gain these we have the same rights as other animals to take what we need. Sometimes that may mean taking other animals' lives, or taking over their living space.

But when we do, we should do so only for vital reasons, and with full respect for the creatures, just as Native Americans honour and ask forgiveness of the animals they hunt. And we should do so in a way that minimizes the suffering for these animals and all others.

Whether they are vegetarians or not, all pantheists would agree that we should choose our diet with consideration for the way in which animals are farmed, and the impact of this on the animals' welfare and the wider environment. This means supporting compassionate farming of livestock: allowing animals like chickens, pigs and cattle freedom to roam and graze, to root and roost, and to rear their offspring in close intimacy. It means encouraging compassionate farming by choosing products that are farmed in this way.

Pantheists are divided on experiments on animals. Some would ban them altogether, while others believe they are essential to the development of medicine and science and justified by the our right to preserve human life. All would agree that experimental methods that avoid animal use should always be preferred where possible, that animal suffering should be minimized, and that no animal experiments should be conducted for non-essential reasons like cosmetic testing.

Preserving the diversity of species and habitats

Environmentalists often talk of the right of species to survive. In moral terms species are categories of living things: they are not sentient beings, they cannot feel pain, distress or fear.

But they can be seen in the same light as we see human ethnic/cultural groups. Although we are all part of one species, we regard an ethnic/cultural group as an important thing to preserve for the sake of the individuals who make it up. In the same way, we should regard species as important for the sake of the individual animals that make them up. There is an international convention against genocide - the deliberate destruction of an ethnic group, either by killing, or by forcing conditions on the group which are likely to bring about its destruction. We need an international convention against genocide practised on animal species.

Individual species are not just important in themselves - they are part of the broader landscape. Each species adds extra variety and complexity to the scene.

The full range of genes, species and habitats is known as biodiversity. Biodiversity is an ethical value in itself for pantheists and for environmentalists more generally. It is crucially important to humans and to all living things. If we reduce the genetic diversity of a species, we reduce its ability to adapt to changing environmental conditions and therefore its vulnerability to extinction - this is why it's important not just to preserve the last few hundred individuals of a species, but as many as possible. Species diversity is also important to ecosystem stability. If we reduce the species diversity of an ecosystem such as a forest or grassland, we increase its vulnerability to climate change.

Species do not exist in a vacuum. They evolve in a habitat, and they depend on their habitat for food, security, and the chance to reproduce. So preserving the diversity of habitats is perhaps the most important measure in preserving the diversity of species, and the stability of the greatest ecosystem of them all, our planet earth.

Nature's also has an immense practical benefit to humans. It provides ecological services such as soil creation and the regulation of climate, and economic benefits such as new crops and new medicines. Not least it is of great aesthetic value: think of the difference between a regimented pine plantation with dark lifeless ground, and a natural forest of oak and birch and ash, with fallen trees and open glades and all the variety of animal life that these sustain.

Our own self-interest, as also our religious reverence for Nature, demand that we should preserve the diversity of species and of habitats in all its richness.

The Earth Ethic

Most Western religions have traditionally accorded a low priority to conserving nature. There are some injunctions in Judaism concerned with leaving the land fallow, and treating animals with kindness. In Islam, born in the fragile environment of Arabia, there is a stronger stress on the rights of animals, and on the need to conserve soil, water and trees.

In the core Christian scriptures, concern for the environment is almost entirely absent. It's true that the New Testament often has a rural setting, and Jesus frequently uses agricultural or natural images that suggest a love of nature. Yet alongside his injunctions to love other humans, he gives us no instructions whatsoever to be kind to animals or to conserve nature. Nor does St Paul. In Jesus' apocalyptic warnings, and in the Book of Revelation, the image of God himself destroying the earth he has created before the Last Judgement, is perhaps not one that encourages respect for nature. In fact some fundamentalists welcome the increasing destruction of our planet as a sign of the impending return of Christ.

Eastern religions are very different in this respect. Perhaps because India and China urbanized earlier than the West, they developed an earlier love of nature. In Buddhism compassion for all living creatures is a central part of the faith. Jainism goes to extreme lengths to avoid harming animals - pious Jains wear face masks to avoid swallowing flies and gently sweep paths in front of them to avoid trampling on beetles and spiders.

As in many other ways, Pantheism more resembles eastern religions in its regard for the environment. Much of the deeper green end of the environmental movement is inspired by pantheistic sentiment. People like Julia Butterfly, who risk their lives to save trees or wildlife, are not driven by abstract philosophical arguments, but by powerful feelings of compassion and value.

Nature herself makes a moral call. People who love Nature feel intensely that all natural things are sacred, and that it is sacrilege to harm them unnecessarily in pursuit of greed, convenience, or fun. They love the whole rich tapestry that nature has taken billions of years to weave, and they want to preserve it against the destructive inroads of pollution and development.

Pantheism has an ecological approach to ethics which is concerned not only with the individual organism or the individual species, but also with the whole community of living and non-living things in which they thrive.

Principles of Deep Ecology

Deep Ecology has an essentially pantheistic reverence for Nature. Norwegian philosopher Arne Naess, one of the founders of the Deep Ecology school, has summed up the basic principles of the school's platform:

1. The well-being and flourishing of human and non-human life on earth have value in themselves. These values are independent of the usefulness of the non-human world for human purposes.

2. Richness and diversity of life forms contribute to the realization of these values and are values in themselves.

3. Humans have no right to reduce this diversity except to satisfy vital needs . . .

4. The flourishing of human life and cultures is compatible with a substantially smaller human population . . .

5. Present human interference with the non-human world is excessive, and the situation is rapidly worsening.

6. Policies must therefore be changed. These policies affect basic economic, technological and ideological structures. The resulting state of affairs will be deeply different from the present.

7. The ideological change will be mainly that of appreciating life quality rather than adhering to an increasingly higher standard of living. There will be profound awareness of the difference between bigness and greatness.

8. Those who subscribe to the foregoing points have an obligation directly or indirectly to try to implement the necessary changes.

US naturalist Aldo Leopold called this approach the Land Ethic:

> *The land ethic simply enlarges the boundaries of the [moral] community to include soils, waters, plants and animals, or collectively, the land . . . A thing is right when it tends to preserve the integrity, stability and beauty of the biotic community. It is wrong when it tends otherwise.*

Today the Land Ethic needs to be broadened to include the coasts, oceans and atmosphere. And the "biotic community" should now include every element of the Gaia system. Today it might be called the Earth Ethic, and rephrased as follows:

> *A thing is right when it tends to preserve the integrity, stability, and diversity of the biotic community at every level of ecosystem up to that of the earth as a whole. It is wrong when it tends otherwise.*

The Earth Ethic is not simply a matter of changing government policies, but of changing the attitudes and behaviour of billions of individual humans, starting with ourselves. Each one of us can affect the environment directly, for good or for bad, through our behaviour as consumers. Through our purchasing choices we can change market demand and affect what kinds of goods are produced. By choosing goods produced in friendly ways, we can help to shift industrial technology. By avoiding unnecessary consumption and waste, we can reduce the pollution we produce.

Respecting human rights

The pantheist attitude to other humans is one of the deepest respect. Humans are not just equal participants in the unfolding of the Universe: every individual consciousness is an equal focus of awareness of nature and the cosmos. Whatever our abilities or disabilities, we are all absolutely equal in this central respect.

We should recognize other humans as equal participants in and observers of the Reality we revere. We should treat them as ends in themselves and not simply as means to our own ends. And we should help to alleviate their suffering where we can.

We should respect their legitimate goals in life. We do not have to draw up a list of these goals from scratch. They have been summarized in what is probably the greatest ethical achievement of our species so far: the body of international human rights. These include civil rights such as freedom of speech, opinion, religion, assembly and association, and freedom from torture and arbitrary detention. They include political rights such as the right to democracy. And they include economic and social rights such as the right to work, to health care and to freedom from hunger.

Recognizing human unity

Just as pantheists believe strongly in the unity of the Cosmos (see page 45) and of Nature (see page 52), they also believe in the unity of the human race. We all share a common origin - recent genetic research suggests that we may all be descended from a single family that lived in Africa some 200,000 years ago.

As with nature and the universe, this unity is not simply a matter of history: it is an everyday reality that has strong ethical consequences. In every society the welfare of the poorest affects the welfare of the whole society: those who are unable to lead a life of dignity often turn to crime. And in every society the environmental actions of one individual or institution impinge on everyone else.

The unity extends to global level. Today the whole world is linked economically - every one of us depends on the prosperity of every other. We all have an interest in helping to avoid economic crisis, and to eradicating poverty in the poorest countries.

The world is one in health terms. We cannot ignore the health problems of poor countries - new diseases or newly resistant strains of old diseases that develop in one country quickly spread world-wide because of travel and tourism. Your health tomorrow may depend on the health of poor Africans or South Asians today.

Finally, the planet is linked environmentally. Your emissions of greenhouse gases and ozone destroying chemicals today will affect my welfare and perhaps even my survival tomorrow. Gas-guzzling limos in the US or Europe may help to make flood victims homeless in Bangladesh, or to drown low-lying islands in the pacific.

Pantheist affirmation of life, body and sex

The major Western religions give life on this earth a low priority. The eternal destiny of the soul is what matters most. There is a long tradition in Christianity and in Theravada Buddhism of regarding the body as a source of evil and its desires - especially its sexual drives - as urges that should be suppressed or resisted.

Pantheism takes the opposite view and teaches full acceptance of life on this earth in a physical body. This is the only life there is or is ever going to be. Pantheism accepts and embraces the body and the earth, life and death, self and other, unity and diversity, in all their dynamic physical reality. Pantheism nurtures the most profound sensuality, an unrepressed sexuality, and the deepest aesthetic appreciation of Nature. It harbours no delusions that could detract from or distract us from the spectacular charisma of earth and universe.

Many pantheists regard body and soul or spirit as aspects of the same inseparable unity. The body is a sacred part of nature. We have a duty to take care of it, to look after our health and fitness.

Sex is one of the body's strongest needs and urges, and the experience of orgasm is one of the deepest mysteries of human existence. When shared, it can be a mystical experience in which the separate self is completely transcended in union with another person. Mind and body, self and other, are completely fused with body and all sense of separation disappears.

In child-bearing partnerships, sex gains additional meaning as the channel of conception through which we link backwards towards the first life on earth, through all the generations of human evolution and human history, and forwards to all human life in the future.

A few pantheistic groups have made sex the centre of their ritual worship. Tantric Buddhists viewed the whole of reality as Buddha and Nirvana. "I have visited in my wanderings shrines and other places," wrote the 12th century poet Saraha, "but I have not seen another shrine like my own body."
Saraha writes lyrically of orgasm:

> *That blissful delight that consists*
> *between lotus and vajra [vagina and penis],*
> *Who does not rejoice there?*
> *It is profound, it is vast.*
> *it is neither self nor other . . .*
> *Even as the moon makes light in black darkness,*
> *So in one moment the supreme bliss removes all defilement.*
> *When the sun of suffering has set,*
> *Then arises this bliss, this lord of the stars.*
> *It creates with continuous creativity . . .*
> *Gain purification in bliss supreme,*
> *For here lies final perfection.*

The English novelist D. H. Lawrence had a profoundly positive and mystical attitude towards sex as part of his pantheistic affirmation of life. "The human body is only just coming to real life," says his heroine Lady Chatterley, "it is really rising from the tomb. And it will be a lovely, lovely life in the lovely universe."

Ethical codes normally set out to provide norms for social behaviour. But there are also many areas of private behaviour where where individual choices (in moderation) often have few consequences for others. These include sexuality, drink, drugs, and gambling.

Traditional religions often have strong codes for many of these areas. Pantheism by and large does not try to legislate for private victimless behaviour.

Many pantheists accept the Wicca principle: "An' it harm none, do as ye will." The presumption is for freedom - but with the important proviso that no harm is done to others. Freedom is a privilege that must be exercised responsibly.

It might sound as if Pantheism is permissive in the extreme, but this is not the case. The principle of no harm to others can be quite demanding. It doesn't involve looking over one's shoulder all the time to see if God is watching. But it does involve careful consideration of others - including other living creatures - in all that we do. Once that responsibility is discharged, then Pantheism offers a broad freedom to be oneself.

7. Pantheist celebration, meditation and mysticism

Religious ceremony takes a wide range of forms and serves a wide range of functions. It plays a role in the lives of communities, of individuals as members of communities, and of individuals in the private context of their daily lives.

- **Calendar customs** mark special dates of the community's calendar, usually ones that mark specific solar or lunar events, or that are important in the history of the religion or nation, or in the life of the founder, or in days sacred to specific deities.
- **Rites of passage** mark significant moments in individual life such as naming a child, puberty, marriage, and death. They do so publicly, so that the individual event gains community recognition.
- **Placatory rituals**: Many religions have ceremonies that amount to magical rituals, aimed at warding off misfortune or attracting good fortune by placating God or the gods, through praise or sacrifice or repetition of rote formulae.
- **Homage rituals**: Ritual can also express more general emotional or belief positions such as submission to God, like the Muslim prostration, or union with God like the Catholic Eucharist, in which the sacred wafer and wine are thought to become the body and blood of Christ.
  Religions also have more personal and individual rituals.
- **Prayer** makes requests of supernatural powers, or asks forgiveness for sins, or expresses gratitude.
- **Meditation** seeks to deepen religious understanding and to calm personal anxieties and stresses.
- **Mysticism** aims to achieve escape from the boundaries of self and blissful union with God, or with whatever is considered the ultimate reality.

The meaning and function of pantheist celebration

Not all pantheists feel the need for ceremony - some people, reacting against conventional religious experience, find that it reminds them too closely of their religion of birth. Other Pantheists have such an intense love for Nature and life that they are driven to express it in a celebratory way.

Pantheist celebration has a very distinct expressive meaning. In the major Western religions the basis of all ritual is the existence of a personal God who knows all our thoughts and actions, who will punish or reward us after our death, and who has the power to make good or bad things happen in our lives. This God watches everything we do and is said to be pleased when we perform rituals to honour him and displeased if we don't.

Pantheists do not believe in a personal thinking God who can hear our prayers, with whom we can plead for good fortune or escape from misfortune. They do not believe in a God outside of nature, who can revoke the laws of nature and change the course of events to suit our needs. Nature and the Universe are the supreme reality and power, and life on earth is the only life.

So in Pantheism celebratory acts are not intended to influence a supernatural power or to change the course of external events. Rather, they are designed to benefit our own thoughts and moods. They deepen our reverence for nature and the universe, and help us muster our individual or communal strength to cope with life's problems and crises.

Most religions have compulsory rituals which must follow a particular form and sequence. The form is laid down in scripture, or prescribed by the religious authorities. By contrast pantheists do not accept that any writings are especially sacred. They do not accept that any section of humans has better access to true pantheism than any other, or any right to dictate ritual to others. Every one of us has direct access to nature and the Universe through our senses and our emotions and through science. Each one of us knows best what expression of our religious feelings works best for us.

Thus pantheist celebration is very much a matter of choice, for individuals or the groups to which they belong. There is no set form and people use their own inspiration to create their own. An exception to this approach are those pagan pantheists who believe in magic, who may feel that specific rituals are needed to get certain results. But belief in magic is unrelated to Pantheism. You can believe in magic without being a pantheist, and vice-versa.

Pantheist celebration is whatever you wish to do in order to express your joy in life, your religious feelings towards nature and the Universe, to deepen your awareness and knowledge of them, and to prepare yourself for dealing with stress or with life in general.

Sacred time, sacred space

Until modern times, most pantheists in the West saw their belief system as a philosophy rather than a religion and paid little heed to developing any approach to celebration. John Toland envisaged that his pantheist circles would start with a sort of formal pantheist catechism, but this was little more than masonic play-acting.

Modern pantheists have a very wide variety of personalized forms of celebration. All that we can do here is to sketch some broad principles and some common practices.

The Pantheist Year In Outline

January 22	Chief Seattle surrenders native land
February 12	Charles Darwin's birthday (1809)
February 17	Giordano Bruno's martyrdom (1600)
March 8	International Women's Day
March 14	Einstein's birthday (1879)
March 20/21	**Spring equinox.**
April 7:	World Health Day
April 20	Marcus Aurelius birthday (121)
April 22	Earth Day.
May 1	May Day/Beltane.
June 5	World Environment Day.
June 20	World Refugee Day
June 20/21	**Midsummer's day.**
July 11	World Population Day
July 12	Thoreau's birthday (1817)
August 9	International Day of Indigenous People
August 12/13	Perseid meteor shower peak.
Sept 22/23	**Autumn equinox.**
October 16	World Food Day
October 31	Halloween/Samhain: day of the dead
November 16	International Day of Tolerance
November 24	Spinoza's birthday (1632)
November 30	John Toland's birthday (1670)
December 10	Human rights day.
December 13/14	Geminid meteor shower peak.
December 21/22	**Yule. Winter solstice**
December 25	Isaac Newton's birthday
December 29	International Day for Biodiversity

The core aim of pantheist celebration is to express our reverence for nature and the Universe, and to strengthen our vision of human life as part of the great natural cycles. Thus the key pantheist ceremonies are at times and places of special significance in those cycles: times of arrival and departure, times of fullness and of transition.

At sunrise, or on rising, for example, many pantheists greet the sun, and at sunset say farewell. They may celebrate full moons - and not just for their beauty. At this time the moon and the sun are on exactly opposite sides of the earth, and their combined effect (as at new moon) creates high spring tides and exerts a stronger pull on everything on earth. It is a good time to remember the impact that tides have on all life along sea coasts.

The most salient times of Pantheist celebration are the solstices and equinoxes which occur at varying times between the 20 and 23 of March, June, September and December (see Appendix Two page 101). Their significance arises from the annual orbit of the earth around the sun. Because the axis on which the earth spins is tilted in the same direction, the part of the earth which is closest to the sun varies according to the season.

At the spring equinox (March 20 or 21) night and day, darkness and light are equal. The earth is edge on to the sun, which at midday stands directly overhead at the equator, about to move into the northern hemisphere. So in the north, the spring equinox is celebrated as the beginning of a new cycle of growth and reproduction in nature. Flowers begin to bud, and animals to have their offspring.

Midsummer is celebrated on June 21. In the northern hemisphere, it is the time when the midday sun stands highest at the Tropic of Cancer, the day when the sun has its maximum power, when seeds are ripening, fruits and baby animals are growing. Many ancient monuments such as Stonehenge were aligned towards the place where the sun would rise at the summer solstice.

The autumn equinox currently falls on September 22 or 23. It is a time when light and dark are equal, when fruits are ripening and young animals reaching the stage of independence, and when the midday sun leaves the northern hemisphere and stands above the equator again, on its way southwards.

The last great transit of the year is the winter solstice on December 21 or 22. This is the longest night, when the midday suns stands lowest in the north hemisphere. From now on days begin to grow longer and nights shorter, so it is celebrated as the true birth of the new year, the beginning of the sun's return journey from the south.

Of course in the southern hemisphere the significance of all these dates are shifted forward by six months.

These seasonal transitions have been celebrated by humans from ancient times, and even Christianity's greatest festivals are based on them directly or indirectly. The date of Christmas is close to the date of the winter solstice, while Easter is linked to the first full moon after the spring equinox. The spring equinox was the traditional time when the great earth gods of the classical world - Attis, Adonis, Osiris - died and were reborn.

Pagans and other pantheists may also celebrate some of the old Celtic quarter days in between the solstices and equinoxes. May Day (Celtic Beltane) was in origin probably a fertility festival celebrated with fires and Maypoles. Halloween (Celtic Samhain) was the eve of the Celtic and Anglo-Saxon New Year, when the souls of the dead were believed to visit their families. Whether pantheists believe in souls that survive death or not, this day can be used for remembering and honouring dead friends, relatives and ancestors.

Other dates that may be specially observed include the peaks of the two largest meteor showers, the Perseids in early August and the Geminids in the second week in December. These are the times when the earth's orbit crosses the orbit of dense clouds of cometary debris. They teach us of our intimate connection with the rest of the solar system and the history of its formation. Much of earth's water, and possibly the building blocks for life, may have come to us on comets and meteors.

Pantheists may also celebrate certain dates of special historical significance. February 17, the day on which the pantheist Giordano Bruno was martyred in Rome in 1600 AD, serves as a day to remember the importance of religious freedom and tolerance. Earth Day (April 22) and World Environment Day (June 5) are also key dates for nature-honouring pantheists.

Do Pantheists pray?

Pantheists do not pray in the conventional sense of prayer to a god: they do not believe there is anyone to hear praise, or to grant requests for favours or mercy. But many pantheists do practice their own equivalent of prayer. Prayer comes in three basic modes: please, thankyou, and sorry.

A "please" prayer, for a pantheist, would amount to expressing a simple hope that events would turn out in one's favour, or a resolution to do one's best. Scientific research has shown that the mind can influence the health of the body by strengthening or weakening the immune system or affecting hormone levels. So a prayer for recovery could be effective, by awakening the body's own powers of self-healing. Even the knowledge that others too are "praying" for you to get better can have a healing effect by boosting morale.

A pantheist "sorry" prayer might be a self-critique for some inconsiderate or selfish act against other people or against Nature.

And a pantheist "thankyou" prayer would express one's gratitude to Nature and the Universe for the gifts of life and joy and beauty. Pantheists know there is no-one listening to the thanks, but they have a natural emotional need to express it.

Heightened perception

An important aspect of personal devotion for pantheists is heightened perception of the world around them. Pantheists believe that this present world is the
only world we will ever witness: therefore it is important to perceive it in its
full richness, diversity, beauty and mystery.

   Children are born pantheists. They see reality unshaped by culture or language. The whole world seems magical to them, full of novelty, mystery and
power. They look at each thing and study its form and texture. They smell it,
feel it, stick it in their mouths. As adults we can all too easily lose that sense
of beauty and mystery, and if we do the world comes to feel drab and over-
familiar.

   Wordsworth's poem, *Ode on Intimations of Immortality*, conveys this
sense of wonder and its loss:

> *There was a time when meadow, grove and stream,*
> *The earth, and every common sight,*
> *To me did seem*
> *Apparelled in celestial light,*
> *The glory and the freshness of a dream . . .*
> *Heaven lies about us in our infancy.*
> *Shades of the prison house begin to close*
> *upon the growing Boy . . . .*
> *At length the Man perceives it die away*
> *And fade into the light of common day.*

   What causes the "prison house" effect? As we acquire language, we begin
to sort our sense perceptions into fixed categories. We see a tree and say
"tree" and think we have dealt with it. We think we know what it's all about,
and after a quick glance we move on. But we have missed all its uniqueness,
the shock of its presence, the numinous nature of its existence.

   We develop a sort of cataract over the eyes, a fog of words and precon-
ceptions and preoccupations. Only the unusual or the shocking sticks out
through the mist and shakes us in our complacency.

   But heaven is still out there to be witnessed: it's just that we have grown
blind to it. For pantheists it is very important to retain, or to regain, this child-
like ability to see things with fresh eyes, as if we have never seen them before.
We must try to sustain our sense of wonder at the world around us.

   Travel is one way of looking at things afresh. When we go to unfamiliar
places or landscapes, almost everyone does for a time look at things more
closely. But we should be able to look at our garden or local park as naively
and attentively as if it were a tropical rainforest or a host of penguins on an
iceberg.

Nature is the best place to see things freshly. Water, clouds, living things are all individualized, all different, all in motion.

There are many ways we can learn to look at the world with fresh eyes. The primary way is to develop our senses and our sensuality. Our primary senses are based in organs of astonishing sophistication. They have evolved over millions of years to improve our survival skills - but they are also our channels for connecting with the real world, for making contact with and appreciating the divinity that surrounds us.

Here are some ideas for developing heightened perception:

- Go into a garden, park or natural area. Look at subtleties of form and colour and texture and motion that you may have over-looked before: the rough bark of trees, the grain of rock, the pattern of veins on a leaf, the sinuous movement of a swan's neck, the sequence of ripples and eddies on a stream. Look at them in their reality, free of words, look at them for what they are independently of you and of human ideas.

Sight dominates and sometimes suppresses our other senses. We must learn to develop our other senses too.

- Close your eyes and develop your hearing: listen to the wind in the leaves, but listen to the different sound that different trees make. Listen to poplar, willow, sycamore. Listen to the variations in birdsong. Notice how a mocking bird never sings the same notes twice. Listen to the stream, but listen to the different components in its sounds.
- Close your eyes and develop your sense of touch. Feel the bark and leaves of different trees, feel the roughness and smoothness of stones, feel the breeze on your cheeks. Lie in the grass like a lizard on a warm stone and feel the sun warm up your body.

Another way to develop our perception is to remember and record what we see.

- If you go into nature, on a walk, walk through it again in your mind before you go to sleep. It's a great way to get to sleep, and rehearsing the memory will preserve it.
- Keep a daily diary of what you see. Trace the sequence of the seasons, the budding and blossoming and fruiting of trees, the courtship and nesting and breeding of animals.
- Describe what is unique about each thing and place and time., Don't use old jaded words and cliches - these are what blind us. Use new words and new metaphors. The recording will deepen your perception. It might even make a poet or novelist of you.

- Draw or paint pictures. Even if you've never done it before, go out with a pad and a soft pencil or water colours and try it. Drawing or painting forces you to study forms, colours and textures with great attention to detail and uniqueness. Start with small things - a rock, a piece of bark, a leaf - and work your way up to whole trees and whole landscapes.
- Take photographs. A photograph is a very special thing. Photons from the sun ricochet from objects on earth, strike the image plane of your camera and alter molecules there. It is reality's self portrait in light. And for you it is a disciplined exercise in the perception of reality. Don't set out to recreate a picture you saw in a magazine or book. Forget every visual cliché you have ever learned. Look for new angles and new times of day that bring out unusual aspects of colour, texture and form.

Heightened awareness

Pantheists can cultivate not just heightened perception of the world, but also of their own physical being in the world. It's all too easy to become totally enmeshed in a web of daily chores, telephones and mail, television and newspapers, traffic jams and bus and tube queues. When that happens we lose almost all awareness of ourselves as natural beings in a natural world.

Pantheism can offer techniques of regaining this awareness to rediscover the sense of wonder at breathing, drinking, eating, exercising, having sex, even going to sleep.

Conscious Breathing
Normally breathing is an involuntary activity which goes on unnoticed in the background, like the quiet hum of a car engine. Yet it is one of the most unifying experiences we can have if we become conscious of it from time to time each day.

Stand at an open window away from traffic, or in a natural area and breathe in, slowly and deeply. Become aware of your breathing at the purely physical level, think of nothing but the act of breathing. And reflect.

At every breath you are taking into our own lungs and bloodstream air that has blown on the winds round the whole earth. With each breath you inhale quintillions of molecules of oxygen which were transpired not just by the trees in the street or garden, but by the forests of the Amazon or the phytoplankton of the southern oceans. You breathe billions of molecules of carbon dioxide that were once emitted by volcanoes in Java or pandas in China.

Long before, this same oxygen and carbon were synthesized in the furnace of an ancient star which exploded as a nova or supernova, scattering its elements across space. Later they would condense again to help make our solar system, and were recycled through all life forms that have ever existed on earth. Every single breath you take contains the history of the galaxy.

Every breath links us with every other human being that ever lived. Astronomer Harlow Shapley once calculated that our every breath contains more than 400,000 of the argon atoms that Gandhi breathed during his lifetime. Argon atoms are here from the conversations of the Buddha. . . and from the recitations of classical poets. We have argon from the sighs and pledges of ancient lovers, and from the battle cries at Thermopylae.

Conscious Drinking

Pour yourself a large glass of cold water and drink it very slowly, feeling it glide down your throat, thinking of nothing but the act of drinking.

Reflect that the water you drink unites you to Gaia just as intimately as the air you breathe. Water too was originally vented by volcanoes, or arrived on fragments of comets, and condensed into seas as the earth cooled. Today it circulates through continual cycles, evaporated from the oceans by the sun, condensing as clouds, and returning through rivers to the sea, passing on the way through countless animals and plants.

The hydrogen in the water was created at the very birth of the universe, as soon as the Big Bang cooled sufficiently for stable atoms to form. So drinking can become a conscious experience of our unity with Gaia and with the history of the universe.

If we learned to breathe and drink in this way at least once a day, we would become very much more concerned to reduce pollution.

Conscious Exercise

Go for a long walk or a run, and think of nothing but the physical act of moving forward. Feel gravity working on you, feel the breeze against your face, feel the tiredness building in your muscles, feel the combinations of muscles shifting almost subconsciously to keep you balanced.

During any form of exercise we can become aware of the action of our muscles working against the gravity that holds us down. Gravity is a universal force holding the earth together, holding us onto the earth, holding the earth to the sun and the sun in the galaxy.

Conscious falling asleep

A good time to do several of these things at once is when you go to sleep every night. Have a long sensuous drink of water. Lie on your back and do conscious slow breathing with your eyes closed. Then turn on side and feel the weight of your body pulled down into the mattress by the earth's gravity, holding you securely like a child in its mother's arms. Feel your own mass and heaviness and tiredness from the day's activity.

Remember and rehearse some simple natural experience of the day or of your life in its sequence and detail. You will feel more deeply grounded and connected, more appreciative of your life in your body on this earth. And you will get to sleep more quickly, sleep more soundly and have sweeter dreams.

Pantheist meditation

Many religions include traditions of meditation. In animistic religions, these are seen as journeys into the world of spirits. In Judaism, Christianity and Islam they are pathways towards union with a creator God, while in Eastern religions or Sufism they may take a much more systematic form as a disciplined sequence of spiritual development.

The practices of heightened perception and heightened awareness described in the last few pages can deliver benefits on a par with those of any other meditation system. They can manage and relieve stress, and bring a personal mental balance and acceptance.

Nature can serve as a perfect setting and object for meditation. Nature can provide a sense of belonging and security. It can offer perspective and release from the problems of our personal lives, making us realize that there is always a ground with which we are always connected, from which we can never be separated.

Certain forms and processes are particularly helpful. What these are for you will depend on your personal taste. I personally find flowing or rippling water, moving clouds, and leaves in wind most powerful in releasing me from the ego and uniting me with what I am observing.

When indoors, away from nature, it can be helpful to use certain physical aids to meditation. Especially natural objects: beautiful pebbles, pieces of bark, large tree seeds, crystals and so on. Smooth beach pebbles are wonderful aids. It is better when these are things you yourself have collected from a natural place you love, because they will have meaning for you linked to the place where you found them.

Focussing intensely on natural forms, or on the natural processes of the body, allows a complete emptying of the mind of all personal concerns and worries.

If it is accompanied by meditation on unity with nature and the universe, it can also place personal problems into a balanced perspective, which can be immensely enriching and strengthening. You were always, are now and always will be a part of the endless creative dance of the cosmos. Nothing can ever happen to you which can deprive you of that belonging.

Pantheist mysticism

Mysticism is the final stage of meditation. Mystics of all religions report strikingly similar experiences: a sense of direct communion with ultimate reality, a sense of complete unity with all things, and a loss of all distinction between self and other. This is often described as "oceanic feeling" or ecstasy, from the Greek *ek-stasis*, standing outside, or being taken out of the self in rapture.

In most religions except Zen and its forerunners in China, this union is portrayed as something extraordinarily difficult to achieve, needing long periods of training and dedication. Often it is seen as something that is attained only very rarely and quickly lost again. The Greek philosopher Plotinus, for example, spent his whole life in search of this feeling of union with divinity, yet he said that he achieved it only once every year or two.

The very word "mystical" reinforces this idea that union is hard to attain. It means something esoteric, occult, hidden, secret. The word derives from mystery, from the Greek word for initiation into secret rites.

Yet these mystical experiences are similar across all religions, from Christianity and Islamic Sufism to Zen or yoga. It's clear that the mystical experience is not dependent on having any special religious doctrine, nor on belief in a God separate from the universe. The sense of union is something that all humans can experience regardless of their particular religion or non-religion.

For Pantheism the ultimate reality is nature and the Universe, and union is union with these. Since these are open for all to see, there is no mystery and no secret. No initiation or arduous training is required. The feeling can be attained at will, on a daily basis, using the techniques described in the previous sections.

Every one of us is at all times surrounded by and immersed in and part of the ultimate reality. The experience of union consists in becoming aware of that unity, losing the self into it, merging mind into body. In this experience the feeling of duality between the world and our personal consciousness vanishes completely. The self enters the universe and the universe enters in to the self, and a feeling of ecstasy can be attained.

8. Pantheist controversies: souls, bodies and death.

No religious path is monolithic. Since humans are all different, different ways of interpretation of the basic principles are continually arising. The budding off of sects is as natural as the branching of trees. Christianity and Buddhism have subdivided into literally hundreds or thousands of different approaches.

Pantheism has never been a united church, so it has never suffered a true schism as such. But it is a very diverse church, and within the diversity there are some major points of difference.

One of these relates to language - specifically, the use of religious terms that are also used by theistic religions. Some pantheists are happy to use words like God, divine, church, ritual and so on. They believe that only words of this import can convey the depth of their religious feelings towards the Universe/Nature.

Others, while sharing these same feelings, prefer to avoid such words, either because they feel personally uncomfortable with them, or because they feel they are misleading to others. It's certainly the case that these terms make most people think of the God of the Jewish, Christian or Islamic scriptures. Any pantheist that uses them has to be prepared to follow them up with an explanation that they mean something different from the most common meanings.

Probably the deepest division relates to the question of whether spirit/soul and matter/body are two separate substances (dualism), or simply aspects of a single substance (monism). Closely related to this is a division over whether the universe is purely physical, or whether it has a spiritual aspect, a kind of cosmic soul or intelligence.

- **Dualistic Pantheism** believes that spirit and matter are two completely different substances, and that the soul is to some extent separate from the body and can survive the body's death.

- **Monistic Pantheism** holds that there is only one fundamental substance. Monism comes in two main varieties.
  Physicalist monism believes that the basic substance is matter/energy, and that mind is a property of matter.
  For **idealist monism**, the one basic substance is mind or consciousness, and matter is simply the product of mind, or even a delusion of mind.

In the East idealist monism is common, and is found in many schools of Buddhism and Hinduism. Physicalist and dualist Pantheisms are the major forms in the West today. We will examine these three schools in turn, beginning with the physicalist version.

Physicalist Pantheism: Reverence for the Physical Universe

Philosophical materialism, today often referred to as physicalism, has nothing whatsoever to do with the sort of materialism that moralists and environmentalists dislike - greedy consumerism and attachment to material possessions. It simply means belief that there is only one basic form of substance, matter/energy. The idea of what matter is has changed over time, and usually means: whatever science considers as material. This includes all forms of energy, anti-matter, as well as invisible forces and fields known through their measurable effects, and as yet unidentified forms of matter such as "dark matter."

The physicalist form of Pantheism has been known under many different names. Scientific Pantheism, religious naturalism, religious Humanism, religious atheism, positive atheism, materialist monism, cosmotheism - all these are extremely similar if not identical in their basic beliefs.

Scientific, physicalist Pantheism is close to the roots of Western Pantheism, in the early Greek philosophers from Thales to Heraclitus. Zeno, the founder of the Stoics, thought that it was totally impossible that something incorporeal could have any effects: "Only a body is capable of acting or being acted upon." The Stoics believed that the soul was a very refined form of matter.

It is also close to the thought of John Toland, who coined the word pantheist. Toland believed that the brain was the cause of the soul, of thoughts and sensations: "All ideas are corporeal," he wrote.

Modern physicalism does not usually take such a simple view. Clearly, there are experiences called thoughts, and they are not of the same nature as bricks or trees. Even so, they are products of the workings of our physical brains, the inner reflection of physical processes.

Physicalist pantheists believe that we are not distinct from our bodies. We are our bodies and our bodies are us. Some people feel that this approach debases human existence to the level of cells and molecules, but this is not the case. Thought is a property of matter/energy that emerges only with very high levels of organization. And in any case cells and molecules are awesome so there is no question of debasing.

The human brain is the most complex structure we know of in the whole universe. It has an estimated 100 billion neurones - as many as there are stars in a galaxy. Each one has some 10,000 links to others, making perhaps one quadrillion linkages in all - a one with 15 zeros after it.

Equally, matter/energy as understood by modern science is vibrant, mysterious, wonderful stuff. It is very different indeed from Newton's idea of hard little balls bumping around, and from Plato's idea of matter as a chaotic and base raw material waiting for divine ideas to shape it.

In modern physics matter is interchangeable with energy. It is ceaselessly in motion, and infinitely creative in the forms it throws up like bubbles in a lake of lava. If human brains and all their thoughts from Buddha to Einstein are manifestations of matter, then matter is more wonderful than most people have ever imagined.

Although the Stoics were physicalists, they believed that the Universe had a kind of collective soul or spirit which designed things and guided their destiny. This soul was made up of a special refined kind of matter, as was the human spirit. By contrast, modern naturalistic pantheists do not believe in a cosmic soul, mind or intelligence. Along with modern neuroscientists, they hold that all mental activity must have some physical basis. There is no place in the visible universe where memory could be stored or information processed on a cosmic scale.

Thus according to physicalist Pantheism the universe has no mind - but it does have minds. Consciousness and intelligence are part of the universe, in humans and other sentient life forms on earth and other planets. In a sense intelligent beings can be seen as the consciousness of the cosmos, its self-awareness. But that doesn't give us any special role to control or to mould the cosmos, or any right to assume that we are the pinnacle and chief purpose of evolution.

For the physicalist pantheist, the Universe has no purpose or meaning in the human sense of the term. This does not mean that it is senseless or absurd. It simply means that purpose is not a concept that can be applied to the totality of everything that exists. The Universe contains all space and all time, so it could not possibly have any external purpose or meaning. Nor do physicalists believe it has an internal purpose or goal, since for this the universe would need to have a mind.

Equally, they do not believe that human life has any external purpose, imposed on us by a God or cosmic mind. But because humans are conscious, we are able to choose our own purpose in life.

For physicalist pantheists the Universe simply exists. It is a cosmic dance of energy and matter, engaged in a ceaseless process of creation, destruction, and evolution, and we are part of the dance. Physicalist pantheists accept this and celebrate it.

Idealist Pantheism: the "real" world as illusion.

Idealist monist Pantheism is first found in the Hindu Upanishads. As the Sve-tasvatara Upanishad puts it:

> *Now, one should know that Nature is illusion,*
> *And that the Mighty Lord is the illusion maker.*

It is common in Buddhism, which regards the material world as *maya*, a sort of magical trick, or as *sunyatta* (emptiness devoid of "real" objects). Some forms of Buddhism and Yoga have assumed that there is no true physical reality at all, only mind.

In the West the first idealist monists were from the Eleatic school. For the school's founder Xenophanes, God was a changeless, resting unity that had existed and would go on existing for all eternity; one, immortal, all-powerful, all-knowing, utterly unlike humans in shape or thought:

> *Always he remains in the same state, changing not at all,*
> *nor is it fitting for him to move now here now there.*

One could view the eighteenth century philosopher Bishop Berkeley as a kind of idealist pantheist: for him, there was no reality other than ideas in the mind of God.

Dualist Pantheism: separate spirits and bodies

Many modern pantheists in the New Age movement are dualists. They believe there are two distinct basic substances in the Universe: spirit and matter. They usually also believe that the human soul is separate from the body and survives death.

While physicalist Pantheism tends to be pretty uniform, dualist Pantheism takes many forms in the modern world. All we can do here is sketch the most basic ideas with some of the variations.

Because they have the basic pantheist belief in the unity of all things, dualist pantheists often believe that some form of spirit may be present in animals and plants, and in rudimentary form even in rocks. This belief is known as pan-psychism.

Thales of Miletus believed that magnets had souls which explained their movement, while the German naturalist Ernst Haeckel wrote a book, intriguingly titled *Crystal Soul*, tracing psychic activity from rocks up to humans. Of course panpsychic pantheists do not believe that stones or plants actually think thoughts. They tend to define "awareness" at these basic levels as simply responsiveness - to gravity, wind, rain, sun, water and so on.

Panpsychics often apply this idea at higher levels and believe that the universe itself has some kind of collective spirit, soul or intelligence. Because they see spirit and matter as separate substances, they do not face the problem of explaining where this cosmic soul might have its physical seat. Many believe that the spirits of all intelligent beings, all animals and plants, make up a vast collective mind, part of which is present in each individual - like Carl Gustav Jung's "collective unconscious."

Many dualist pantheists also believe that the universe may have some kind of conscious purpose or direction. This is usually seen as the progress of evolution towards more and more complex and intelligent life forms which are increasingly linked to one another through communication. The French Jesuit palaeontologist Teilhard de Chardin (1881-1955) was the strongest proponent of this view. Teilhard saw the cosmos advancing, through the emergence of life and the biosphere, to human intelligence and the linking of minds in what he called the "noosphere." This process would end with a focussing of all things and all consciousness in what he called the Omega Point, the culmination of cosmic history in a final unity with God.

Frequently humans are seen as having an obligation to help the universe along towards its goal. The German philosopher Hegel believed that the World-Spirit developed through human actions. The problem with this belief is that it is impossible to decide what the cosmic purpose really is, if any. Some pantheists today believe that we should hasten the next steps in upwards evolution, through genetically engineered humans, self-designing intelligent robots, or human-machine combinations. Other pantheists regard these technologies as unnatural and dangerous.

Among those who believe that spirit is separate from matter, belief in extra-sensory perception, out-of-body voyaging, and even magic is not uncommon. However, these beliefs cross all religious boundaries and are not specifically linked to dualist Pantheism.

Deaths, natural and unnatural

The split between physicalist and dualist Pantheism extends into the afterlife. Scientific, physicalist pantheists believe in natural death and recycling or our elements, while dualists tend often to believe in reincarnation.

For physicalists, spirit is a manifestation of the body and the brain. It follows that the soul is not a separate entity that can detach itself from the body or survive the death of the body.

Thus physicalist or scientific pantheists believe that we do not survive as an individual conscousness after our death - not as ghosts, nor as spirits flying to heaven or awaiting reincarnation in a new body. They believe that in death, as in life, we remain a part of nature and the universe. When we are buried or cremated, our elements are returned to nature. Some join the atmosphere, and ride on the winds. Others become soil and are absorbed into other living things.

The Book of Chuang Tzu recounts the tale of Tzu Lai who was visited on his deathbed by his friend Tzu Li.

> *"Great is the Creator!" said Tzu Li. "What will he make of you now? Will he make you into a rat's liver? Will he make you into an insect's leg?'*
> *Tzu-Lai replied: "The universe gave me my body so I may be carried, my life so I may work, my old age so I may repose, and my death so I may rest. To regard life as good is the way to regard death as good. . . . . If I regard the universe as a great furnace and creation as a master foundryman, why should anywhere I go not be all right?"*

"Every part of me," wrote Marcus Aurelius, "will be reduced by change into some part of the universe, and that part again will change into another part of the universe, and so on forever."

This view of death does not mean that as individuals we disappear without trace. We survive in ways that everyone is familiar with and that no-one of any religious belief denies. Our genes, the basic information codes that make us what we are, live on through our children and close relatives. We live on through the traces of our actions, the things we have created, and through the memories we leave in those who knew us.

These forms of survival are quite enough to satisfy the physicalist, naturalistic pantheist. They can be boosted in pantheist families by keeping family genealogies, with brief histories of every ancestor, and the passing down of heirlooms - treasured possessions that meant something in the dead person's life.

Acceptance of death is an essential part of scientific, naturalistic Pantheism. Death evolved for a purpose. Simple one-celled organisms like bacteria do not die of old age. Unless they are physically destroyed, they clone themselves, by dividing and multiplying. Death made its first appearance with many-celled organisms that reproduce sexually. At each generation the genes are recombined, creating new variations some of which are better adapted to their environment.

So sex and death come as a package: they are mechanisms to help speed along the evolution of a species. Without death there would be no sex, no birth, no parenting, no family warmth. Death is the price we pay for love and joy.

Natural funerals

Many pantheists find great comfort in the idea that when they die, their elements and energy will melt and merge into the nature that they love, and will enable new life to emerge.

Of course if we really do wish to become part of nature when we die, then the character of our funeral arrangements are very important and we must plan for them ahead of time. If we are pumped full of formaldehyde, a dangerous carcinogen, and buried in an expensive hardwood and metal casket, then our very last impact on earth will be destructive and environmentally damaging.

For the sake of the planet as well as of our own peace of mind, we need a return to natural ways. To avoid environmental damage, coffins should be minimal - cardboard or wicker baskets from sustainable managed sources, or simply linen shrouds. Cremation returns many of our elements to the atmosphere, while our ashes can be buried in a favourite place, or scattered on a stream or on the wind.

Many pantheists and pagans would prefer to be buried in natural places, at sea, or in permanent pastures, woodlands or orchards, where their elements can return into the natural cycle. Memorial plaques can be attached to trees near the bodies.

There is a growing movement of woodland burial grounds, which combine pantheist practice with sound environmental sense. Such woodlands can act as refuges for wildlife and help to increase biodiversity, and in a warming greenhouse earth, they increase tree cover and soak up carbon dioxide. Where such burial grounds are in short supply, pantheists, pagans and nature-lovers can club together to buy plots of land and create them.

If you wish to have a natural death and funeral, you must take control of the death process while you are still capable. If you leave it till you are incapacitated, the logic of the medical and funeral industries and of the dominant religious culture will take over and ensure an unnatural death and burial.

The UK-based Natural Death Centre has produced a series of suggested legal forms so that people can state their wishes in advance. They also produce the excellent Natural Death Handbook, with practical guidance and contacts on all aspects of dying, care of the death, green funerals, grieving and so on (see list of contacts at the back of this book).

A Living Will sets out how you wish to be treated medically in case of terminal illness or total incapacity - stating, for example, under what circumstances you would or would not wish medical intervention to prolong your life, and whether you want to be allowed to die at home.

Advanced Funeral Wishes state your preferences about organ donation, embalming, coffin type, bearers, place of burial and funeral ceremony. This can allow you to plan your own funeral as Egyptian pharaohs used to.

Reincarnation?

Dualist pantheists usually believe that we do have an individual afterlife. However, they are still pantheists - they equate God with the universe and nature - so they tend not to believe in Heaven or Hell, separate spirit worlds set aside for us after our death. There may be more than one life, but for them too, there is only one earth, and it is on earth that our future lives will take place.

As pantheists they also share the pantheist affirmation of life on earth in the body. They do not share the Theravada Buddhist view that life is basically suffering, and that reincarnation is something to be dreaded and avoided if at all possible. They positively welcome the idea of reincarnation as a chance to return to this beautiful beloved earth.

"I know I am deathless," wrote the American pantheist poet Walt Whitman. "Round and round we go, all of us, and ever come back hither . . . Births have brought us richness and variety. And other births have brought us richness and variety."

Dualist or physicalist?

Choosing between the three major forms of Pantheism is a matter of personal inclination and conviction.

Not many people in the West today adhere to the idealist form. It cannot explain why - if the world is illusion - we should all seem to share the same illusion. And it is not an approach that can be easily put into practice. Everyone lives *as if* the real world exists. Even idealist pantheists eat and drink and sleep. They cross bridges that stay up; they catch planes that stay airborne. If we consider the idea that there is a real physical world, out there independent of our thoughts, as a very general kind of scientific hypothesis, then it is a theory that checks out very impressively. It probably has more evidence to back it up, and more kinds of evidence, than any more specific scientific theory in existence.

The major rivalry in the West has been between physicalist and dualist Pantheisms. Some thinkers have tried to solve the conflict by supposing that there is just one underlying substance which has both physical and spiritual expressions. Giordano Bruno and Spinoza both favoured this approach. Unfortunately it has not brought an end to the debate. Critics see it as basically ducking the issue or even as adding a third basic substance, just as invisible and undetectable as spirit, to the other two.

Is it possible to resolve the issue one way or the other?

No dualist philosopher has ever succeeded in explaining through what channels or mechanisms spirit effects changes in matter. Physicalists would argue that experience and scientific evidence both suggest strongly that mind is a property of matter. Brain scanning is showing that different types of mental activity are associated with different patterns of activity in the brain. When certain parts of the brain are damaged in accidents or removed in surgery, the corresponding mental faculties weaken or disappear. When we take psychotropic substances such as alcohol or drugs, our mental functioning changes radically.

In nature we can trace the evolution of nervous systems from the hydra, which has a simple neural network without a center, right up to primates with complex brains, and we can see the increase in function along with this evolution. The same paralleling in the growth of mental function and of physical structure can be seen in the development of the human embryo.

Dualists don't deny that the spirit operates through, or in parallel, with the body, but they would argue that the soul exists on a different plane and so would never register on scientific instruments. They point to the increasing number of Near Death Experiences, now that medical technology has made resuscitation possible even after periods of "death" extending up to half an hour.

Of course, physicalists offer naturalistic explanations for these same phenomena. Psychologist Susan Blackmore argues that they can be explained by physical and perceptual processes in the dying, oxygen-starved brain, and by our natural impulse to impose sense and meaning on experience. It can also be argued that anyone who comes back to life before bodily decay has set in has not really died. No-one has been buried for weeks or cremated and returned from the dead.

The debate is unlikely to die down soon. Whether it is really distinct from the body or not, mind does *appear* to be distinct, and this will always tempt people to assume that it really *is* distinct. And our natural instinct to survive attracts many people to the idea of a personal life beyond the grave.

In all probability the debate will continue for a very long time, at least until computers reach the level of human intelligence and awareness - or until neuroscience can offer a more complete physical explanation of our thought processes.

9: A fifth world spiritual path?

Towards the end of the nineteenth century Pantheism seemed to have gained an unstoppable momentum. But in the twentieth century this thrust was abruptly halted, and it was only in the closing decades of the century that something of the old promise seemed to be returning.

Why did the slowdown happen? The nineteenth century in the West was one of unbounded optimism, faith in science and technology, and extended peace in Europe. The twentieth century was a much gloomier era in which disaster, fear, and depths of human degradation followed close on one another's heels. World War One, the Russian revolution, Stalinism, Fascism, World War Two, the Holocaust, the Chinese revolution: all these traumatic upheavals were accompanied by millions upon millions of deaths and massive movements of refugees, most of them associated in one way or another with the struggle of all-embracing political ideologies. Under these circumstances most creative minds were focussed on politics, ideology and sheer survival.

Then came the cold war with its constant fear of nuclear conflict. In the wake of the failure of all-embracing ideologies, post-war intellectual trends moved away from the idea that there could be simple universal truths valid for everyone. Existentialism taught that each person must make their own choice of destiny in order to be "authentic." It was the basic fact of choosing any specific destiny, rather than the nature of the choice, that mattered, so in one sense all choices were equally valid.

Post-modernism, which became a dominant discourse in humanities courses, undermined the idea of universal messages or meanings. Any belief system was all right if it worked for you, and the possibility of any objective yardstick was denied. Even science came to be viewed by many people with tremendous distrust or hostility, as if it were not a proven discipline for arriving closer to the truth, but just another belief system, with no greater claim to truth than astrology or alchemy. Meanwhile pure science was blamed for every monstrosity that technology created, from nuclear bombs to "chimera" animals combining separate species.

A pantheist renaissance?

From the 1960s onwards the outlook for Pantheism became gradually more favourable. The baby-boomer generation born in the West after the end of World War Two had not witnessed mass trauma, and developed a more positive attitude to life. The flower-power generation was at bottom pantheistically inclined, affirming life on this earth in the body. From the seventies onwards, mounting environmental problems created a growing concern for nature and acknowledgement of its value.

As the twenty first century opened, the world moved backwards into another period of insecurity and conflict. To a considerable extent this revolved - for the first time since the seventeenth century - around religious convictions, of fundamentalist Moslems, Jews, and Christians. This development was self-reinforcing, in that as conflict deepened, more people were attracted to the extremes to seek retaliation. Fuelling all these groups, making them willing to risk death for their convictions, was the belief that they alone knew God's will, and that He would reward them in the afterlife.

And yet the frontline fighters were everywhere only a tiny minority, while in the background growing majorities were able to see more clearly the dangerous consequences of fundamentalism of all kinds.

Pantheism offers a gentler alternative. It is now making powerful inroads in the West. Religions with a pantheistic or nature-oriented outlook are expanding - Taoism, Zen and Hua Yen Buddhism, paganism. Deep Ecology fostered a quasi-religious attitude to nature, and environmentalists increasingly spoke of the spiritual foundation of their concerns.

Meanwhile trends in science moved away from a purely mechanistic, purely reductionist view to a more holistic understanding of levels of complexity in the universe. In the face of the mysteries of quantum physics and cosmology, simple unadorned atheism no longer seemed sufficient as a religious philosophy. Increasing numbers of scientists, while rejecting a personal God, spoke of their profound reverence and awe at the wonders of the cosmos and their feeling that nature is sacred.

It is difficult to estimate the numbers of people in the world today who are essentially pantheists in their orientation, but we can make a very rough attempt using some reasonable assumptions. Very conservatively, we could estimate 1-2% of the 2.1 billion Christians; 5-10% of the 850 million Hindus; 10% of the 370 million Buddhists; 10-20% of 940 million atheists, humanists and non-religious and 30% of the 100 million New Religionists.[1] This would put the pantheist total at somewhere between 200 and 350 million. If this is anywhere near the true figure, Pantheism would already rank fourth or fifth among world spiritual orientations today, after Christianity, Islam, Hinduism, and possibly Buddhism. Of course, most of these millions would not use the term pantheist. But they would share a common feeling that nature and the Universe were the prime focus for religious reverence, rather than a personal creator God who was wholly or partly separate from the world.

Organized Pantheism?

For the foreseeable future the greatest growth in pantheist numbers is likely to come as more and more people from traditional religions shift to a pantheistic interpretation of the faith they were raised in. We saw in chapters two and three how the fundamental scriptures of most of the world's religions contain seeds which could grow into such a blossoming.

Pantheistic trends are gaining ground inside Christianity. Movements like the US-based Creation Spirituality talk of a God that is totally immanent in nature. Set up by the defrocked Dominican priest Matthew Fox, Creation Spirituality reinterprets Christian words and symbols in a highly pantheistic way (though Fox claims to be a panentheist rather than a pantheist.)

Increasingly, however, Pantheism will emerge from the fringes of other faiths and appear as a spiritual path in its own right, under its own name, and using its own natural vocabulary and ceremony rather than those inherited from ancient religions of the past.

At present, people who openly call themselves pantheists are disorganized and split into many different groupings. Pagans are the largest group in numbers, but there is no standardized set of beliefs - most pagans would regard such a thing as anathema. And there is no organized pagan church - people come together in informal local groupings, each with their own rituals.

There is some disagreement among Pantheists about whether Pantheism should be organized or not. Pantheists tend to be independent-minded people who have rejected their parental religion. In the United States especially, they have a negative image of religious organizations, based on the aggressive activities of fundamentalist Christians and other cults.

On the other hand, if Pantheism is to become available as a spiritual option to the wider majority, it must organize so as to make itself known as an option, and to offer pantheists the chance of getting together.

There are two organizations specifically for pantheists. The Universal Pantheist Society was founded in California by Harold Wood and Derham

---

[1] The totals are based on figures from the World Evangelization Research Center

Giuliani in 1975. It has no statement of beliefs, and accepts all the diverse types of pantheist, dualist, physicalist and idealist, mentioned in chapter eight. Because of this, when educating the public about what Pantheism is, the UPS can only outline the most rudimentary basic belief in the divinity of the Universe and nature.

The largest pantheist organization is the World Pantheist Movement, founded by the present author and colleagues in 1998. It promotes a physicalist type of Pantheism also known as Scientific or Natural Pantheism. Its central belief statement is presented in the Appendix. This statement is not intended as dogma or required belief, but simply as guidance for prospective members.

The World Pantheist Movement has almost 60 email groups for various interests and for local areas. It has a strong focus not just on love and care for nature but on active conservation of nature. Working with EcologyFund it has organized an on-line group which has saved many acres of wildlife habitat (the conservation is paid for by advertisement sponsors, of which the World Pantheist Movement is also one). It also encourages members to declare wildlife habitat reserves on land they control.

The ultimate aim of organizing Pantheism is to place Pantheism on an equal footing with every other recognized religion and spiritual approach, in terms of public information, local meetings, and people's right to have weddings and funerals in accordance with their beliefs.

The first goal is to provide information about Pantheism as widely as possible, so that people have the option to choose Pantheism among all the other spiritual approaches on offer. This is not the same as "proselytizing." By its very nature Pantheism cannot make psychological threats to gain members. It cannot threaten God's punishment on unbelievers; it cannot promise Heaven to the faithful. All it can ever do is to provide information about its basic beliefs, and point out the personal and social advantages of those beliefs.

A second key aim is to promote the growth of local groups, so that pantheists have the chance to get together with like-minded folk for mutual society and support, just like people of other spiritual paths do, and to develop together their understanding and connection with nature and the Universe. Getting together in groups is a basic human urge, and in the case of minority beliefs it can be important for morale. In many countries, pantheists often find themselves isolated and sometimes victimised. Meeting fellow pantheists can mean a lot in terms of support and personal morale.

Finally there is a need for a network of pantheist celebrants and counsellors. The "theology" of Pantheism ensures that this could never mean a hierarchy of holy priests blessed by high religious leaders. When everyone can have direct access to the pantheist "divinity" at any time, no-one can claim higher authority or the right to mediate or dictate.

Yet there are key times in life when the assistance of an experienced person who shares one's spiritual outlook may be needed - to provide counselling in cases of terminal illness, bereavement and other major life problems, for example. Or to help hold ceremonies for child-naming, weddings or funerals. Such passages are among the most important experiences in life, and everyone wants ceremonies that are in keeping with their deepest beliefs.

Many pantheists today design their own personal ceremonies, but not everyone feels capable of this - especially in the case of funerals, when they are coping with grief and practical and legal arrangements as well. If pantheists do not have their own options available, then they will often be forced to fall back on ceremonies of other faiths that inwardly they may find meaningless or even distasteful.

Future growth potential

Future trends seem likely to favour the further growth of Pantheism, either under its own name or in the form of increasingly pantheistic versions of other religions.

Trends in the religious sphere are favouring the emergence of a common spiritual basis for all religions, in which individual religious traditions are seen as different ways of celebrating the same ultimate reality. Most countries in the world today, at least in the West, are multicultural and multi-religious. It is now impossible for anyone to ignore the existence of other religions in their own back yard, and it is more and more difficult to dismiss other people's religions as nothing but misguided folly. Increasingly, spirituality is coming to be seen as a matter of personal choice, and this is bound to loosen the bonds of traditional religions.

Religions are also engaging in multi-faith dialogue - partly to confront global problems of environment, development and human rights, partly to find ways of living with each other peacefully. This too has encouraged a sort of generalized spirituality based on shared human experiences and values. It has brought theistic religions like Judaism, Christianity and Islam into dialogue with non-theistic religions like Buddhism or Taoism. Because Buddhists and philosophical Taoists do not believe in a personal God, the declarations that come out of inclusive inter-faith meetings make no reference to God. They usually express care and concern about nature, and embody a basic set of human ethics that is common to most religions.

The world's environmental problems will mount in severity for at least several more decades. We are losing more and more species and natural habitat to pollution, deforestation, over-exploitation and development. Awareness of these problems is already leading to a widespread revolution in human values towards the natural world and to other species. As traditional religions try to reinterpret and re-evaluate their founding scriptures in the light of the need to save nature and the planet, a spiritual approach that makes this project its central focus is bound to seem attractive.

Increasing educational levels all over the world are another factor favouring change. The more education people have, the less ready they are to accept traditional beliefs on the basis of scriptural or priestly or parental authority.

Meanwhile science continues to push back the frontiers of explanation, leaving a smaller and smaller space for supernatural action by a God outside the universe.

At the same time telescopes like the Hubble are revealing more and more of the breathtaking power and violence and beauty of the universe. More and more stars are being discovered with planetary systems, and the possibilities of discovering life beyond earth are widening. Yet to some extent science's advances into deeper territories is increasing, rather than reducing, the reasons to feel awe and wonder at Nature and the Universe.

In the first centuries of our era, Pantheism was the leading religious philosophy from the Roman Empire across to China. In the nineteenth century it represented the vanguard of religious debate in the West. At the opening of the new millennium it is possible to foresee a time when Pantheism may regain some of its old prominence and move towards the status of a world spiritual path.

Appendix One:
The Pantheist Credo

The Pantheist Credo is the first attempt, as far as is known, to create a basic outline statement of pantheist beliefs. It was drawn up and agreed by a working group of fifteen members of the World Pantheist Movement e-mail list (to join the WPM see details at the end of this book) The group completed their work in December 1997 and the credo has been revised twice since then.

The Pantheist Credo is not like the creed of any brand of Christianity. There is no compulsion to agree to it. Basically it is intended as a succinct statement for members of the World Pantheist Movement, and a guide for people who are thinking of joining.

It is a belief statement for the scientific, naturalistic, physicalist strand of Pantheism sometimes known as religious naturalism, religious atheism or religious Humanism. Almost all pantheists would assent broadly to clauses 1, 2, 3, 4, 8 and 9. Some might have alternative approaches to mind/body and death as covered in 5, 6 and 7.

The Pantheist Credo

1. We revere and celebrate the Universe as the totality of being, past, present and future. It is self-organizing, ever-evolving and inexhaustibly diverse. Its overwhelming power, beauty and fundamental mystery compel the deepest human reverence and wonder.

2. All matter, energy, and life are an interconnected unity of which we are an inseparable part. We rejoice in our existence and seek to participate ever more deeply in this unity through knowledge, celebration, meditation, empathy, love, ethical action and art.

3. We are an integral part of Nature, which we should cherish, revere and preserve in all its magnificent beauty and diversity. We should strive to live in harmony with Nature locally and globally. We acknowledge the inherent value of all life, human and non-human, and strive to treat all living beings with compassion and respect.

4. All humans are equal centers of awareness of the Universe and nature, and all deserve a life of equal dignity and mutual respect. To this end we support and work towards freedom, democracy, justice, and non-discrimination, and a world community based on peace, sustainable ways of life, full respect for human rights and an end to poverty.

5. There is a single kind of substance, energy/matter, which is vibrant and infinitely creative in all its forms. Body and mind are indivisibly united.

6. We see death as the return to nature of our elements, and the end of our existence as individuals. The forms of "afterlife" available to humans are natural ones, in the natural world. Our actions, our ideas and memories of us live on, according to what we do in our lives. Our genes live on in our families, and our elements are endlessly recycled in nature.

7. We honor reality, and keep our minds open to the evidence of the senses and of science's unending quest for deeper understanding. These are our best means of coming to know the Universe, and on them we base our aesthetic and religious feelings about reality.

8. Every individual has direct access through perception, emotion and meditation to ultimate reality, which is the Universe and Nature. There is no need for mediation by priests, gurus or revealed scriptures.

9. We uphold the separation of religion and state, and the universal human right of freedom of religion. We recognize the freedom of all pantheists to express and celebrate their beliefs, as individuals or in groups, in any non-harmful ritual, symbol or vocabulary that is meaningful to them.

Appendix Two:
A Pantheist and Pagan Almanac 2003-2010

Equinoxes and Solstices
Full moons
Principal Meteor Showers.
Major conjunctions

Regular astronomical events underline the cycle of our connection with the solar system as members of a larger universe. Reverent Naturalists, Pantheists and pagans like to celebrate these events. For many people, simply marking the day is sufficient - but an extra level of inner intensity can be gained by observing the exact time and reflecting on the astronomical significance of the moment for earth's place in the cosmos.

This almanac provides the timing for many of these events. All times are given in Universal Time [Greenwich Mean Time]. This is, eg, five hours ahead of standard time in New York, eight hours ahead of San Francisco, two hours behind Johannesburg, ten hours behind Sydney. Adjustments must be made for daylight saving times - please check out your local arrangements.

Equinoxes and Solstices

2003

Spring equinox	March 21	01 00
Summer solstice	June 21	19 10
Autumn equinox	September 23	10 47
Winter solstice	December 22	07 04

2004

Spring equinox	March 20	06 49
Summer solstice	June 21	00 57
Autumn equinox	September 22	16 30
Winter solstice	December 21	12 42

2005

Spring equinox	March 20	12 34
Summer solstice	June21	06 46
Autumn equinox	September22	22 23
Winter solstice	December 21	18 35

2006

Spring equinox	March 20	18 26
Summer solstice	June 21	12 26
Autumn equinox	September 23	04 03
Winter solstice	December 22	00 22

2007

Spring equinox	March 21	00 07
Summer solstice	June 21	18 06
Autumn equinox	September 23	09 51
Winter solstice	December 22	06 08

2008

Spring equinox	March 20	05 48
Summer solstice	June 20	23 59
Autumn equinox	September 22	15 44
Winter solstice	December 21	12 04

2009

Spring equinox	March 20	11 44
Summer solstice	June 21	05 45
Autumn equinox	September 22	21 18
Winter solstice	December 21	17 47

2010

Spring equinox	Mar 20	17 32
Summer solstice	June 21	11 28
Autumn equinox	Sept 23	03 09
Winter solstice	Dec 21	23 38

Full Moons

2003		2004	
January 18	10 48	January 7	15 40
February 16	23 51	February 6	08 47
March 18	10 34	March 6	23 14
April 16	19 36	April 5	11 03
May 16	03 36	May 4	20 33
June 14	11 16	June 3	04 20
July 13	19 21	July 2	11 09
August 12	04 48	July 31	18 05
September 10	16 36	August 30	02 22
October 10	07 27	September 28	13 09
November 9	01 13	October 28	03 07
December 8	20 37	November 26	20 07
		December 26	15 06
2005		2006	
January 25	10 32	January 14	09 48
February 24	04 54	February 13	04 44
March 25	20 58	March 14	23 35
April 24	10 06	April 13	16 40
May 23	20 18	May 13	06 51
June 22	04 14	June 11	18 03
July 21	11 00	July 11	03 02
August 19	17 53	August 9	10 54
September 18	02 01	September 7	18 42
October 17	12 14	October 7	03 13
November 16	00 57	November 5	12 58
December 15	16 15	December 5	00 25
2007		2008	
January 3	13 57	January 22	13 35
February 2	05 45	February 21	03 30
March 3	23 17	March 21	18 40
April 2	17 15	April 20	10 25
May 2	10 09	May 20	02 11
June 1	01 04	June 18	17 30
June 30	13 49	July 18	07 59
July 30	00 48	August 16	21 16
August 28	10 35	September 15	09 13
September 26	19 45	October 14	20 02
October 26	04 52	November 13	06 17
November 24	14 30	December 12	16 37
December 24	01 16		

2009		2010	
January 11	03 27	January 30	06 18
February 9	14 49	February 28	16 38
March 11	02 38	March 30	02 25
April 9	14 56	April 28	12 18
May 9	04 01	May 27	23 07
June 7	18 12	June 26	11 30
July 7	09 21	July 26	01 36
August 6	00 55	August 24	17 05
September 4	16 03	September 23	09 17
October 4	06 10	October 23	01 36
November 2	19 14	November 21	17 27
December 2	07 30	December 21	08 13
December 31	19 13		

Meteor Showers.

Meteors are tiny fragments of comet and asteroid, which enter the earth's atmosphere as the earth crosses the orbit of the parent body which left them behind as debris, and burn up in a spectacular light show.

The showers are best observed from rural areas without street lighting.

Perseids

This summer shower is linked to the comet Swift Tuttle. At their peak, the Perseids appear to radiate from RA=47 deg, DECL=+57 deg in the constellation of Perseus.

Period:	July 23 to August 22
Peak:	August 12-13
Peak rate:	Average 80 per hour.

Geminids

These first appeared in 1862 and are linked to the asteroid 3200 Phaethon which has an earth-crossing orbit. At their peak, these radiate from RA=112.5 deg, DEC=+32.6 deg in the constellation Gemini.

Period: December 6-19	
Peak:	December 13-14
Peak rate:	Average 80-100 per hour.

Data sources:

Solar and lunar data:	US Naval Observatory.
Meteor data:	American Meteor Society.

Appendix Three:
Useful Contacts & Resources

World Pantheist Movement
P.O. Box 103
Webster, NY 14580
United States.
Website:
http://www.pantheism.net/index.htm
e-mail: info@pantheism.net
Natural Pantheism website:
http://members.aol.com/Heraklit1/index.htm

HUUmanists/Friends of Religious Humanism,
c/o The American Humanist Association
PO Box 1188,
Amherst,
New York 1422607188,
United States.
Web site: http://www.americanhumanist.org/hsfamily/huumanist.html
e-mail: huumanists@americanhumanist.org

The Natural Death Centre,
20, Heber Road,
London NW2 6AA,
United Kingdom.
Web site: http://www.globalideasbank.org/natdeath.html
e-mail: rhino@dial.pipex.com
[See NDC Web site for contacts in North America.]

The Pagan Federation,
BM Box 7097,
London WC1N 3XX,
United Kingdom.
Web site: http://www.paganfed.demon.co.uk/
e-mail: secretary@paganfed.demon.co.uk

Unitarian Universalist Association,
25, Beacon Street,
Boston,
Massachusetts MA 02108,
United States.
Web site: http://www.uua.org/
e-mail: info@uua.org

The Universal Pantheist Society,
PO Box 265,
Big Pine,
California CA 93513,
United States.
Web site: http://users.aol.com/pansociety/index.html
e-mail: pansociety@aol.com

Resources on the Internet:

World Pantheism:
        http://www.harrison.dircon.co.uk/wpm/index.htm

Natural pantheism (pantheist theory, practice and history:
        http://members.aol.com/Heraklit1/index.htm

Pantheist mailing lists:
        http://www.pantheism.net/communit.htm

Usenet newsgroup (for all-in discussion about pantheism):
        news:talk.religion.pantheism

General pantheist links on the Web:
        http://members.aol.com/PHarri5642/pantmark.htm

Hubble Space Telescope
        http://www.stsci.edupubinfo/SubjectT.html

Essential Reading on Pantheism.

Wherever possible cheap recent paperback editions are mentioned. In some cases the US and UK publishers of the same book may be different.

1. Introduction
Harrison, Paul, Scientific Pantheism, including the theory and history of Pantheism with extensive biographies and text extracts. Web site URL: http://members.aol.com/Heraklit1/index.htm
Levine, Michael, Pantheism, Routledge, London and New York, 1994.
Harvey, Graham and Hardman, Charlotte, Paganism Today, Thorsons, London 1996.
Adler, Margot, Drawing Down the Moon, Penguin Books, New York, 1997.

2. History: Oriental and Classical
Hinduism:
Hume, Robert, The Thirteen Principal Upanishads, Oxford University Press (India), 1995.
Edgerton, Franklin, The Bhagavad Gita, Harvard Oriental Series, 1994.
Buddhism:
De Bary, William, ed., The Buddhist Tradition, Vintage Books, New York, 1972.
Kalupahana, David, Nagarjuna, State University of New York Press, 1986.
Mookerjee, Ajit and Khanna, Madhu, The Tantric Way, Thames and Hudson, London, 1977.
Cleary, Thomas, The Flower Ornament Scripture, Shambala, Boulder, 1984.
Cleary, Thomas, Entry into the Inconceivable, University of Hawaii Press, Honolulu, 1983.
Chung Yuan, Chang, Original Teachings of Ch'an Buddhism, Grove Press, New York, 1982.
Suzuki, Daisetz, Essays in Zen Buddhism, Grove Press, New York, 1986.
Taoism:
Schipper, Kristofer, Taoist Body, University of California Press, Berkeley, 1982.
Wu, John, Tao Teh Ching, Shambala, Boston, 1989.
Palmer, Martin, The Book of Chuang Tzu, Penguin Arkana, London and New York, 1996.
Greece and Rome:
Kahn, Charles, The Art and Thought of Heraclitus, Cambridge University Press, Cambridge, 1979.

Long, A. A. & Sedley, D. N., eds, The Hellenistic Philosophers, volume 1, Cambridge University Press, Cambridge, 1987.
Barnes, Jonathan, Early Greek Philosophy, Penguin, London and New York, 1987.
Marcus Aurelius, Meditations, Penguin, London and New York, 1969.
Lucretius, On the Nature of the Universe, trs R. E. Latham, Penguin, London and New York, 1994.
Plotinus, The Enneads, ed John Dillon, Penguin, London and New York, 1991.

3. History: Monotheist and modern
Judaism:
Cohen, A., Everyman's Talmud, Schocken Books, New York, 1975
Scholem, Gershom, Kabbalah, Meridian, London and New York, 1974.
Matt, Daniel, The Essential Kabbalah, Castle Books, Edison, 1997.
Islam:
Ibn Arabi, The Bezels of Wisdom, SPCK, London, 1980.
Massignon, Louis, Al Hallaj, ed. Herbert Mason, Princeton University Press, Princeton, 1994.
Christianity:
Meister Eckhart, Selected Writings, translated by Oliver Davies, Penguin Books, London and New York, 1994.
Jakob Boehme, The Way to Christ, trs w. Zeller, Paulist Press, New York, 1978.
Post-Christian:
Bruno, Giordano, Cause, Principle and Unity, ed., Richard Blackwell, Cambridge University Press, Cambridge, 1998.
Spinoza, Benedict, A Spinoza Reader, Princeton University Press, Princeton, 1994.
Toland, John, Pantheistikon, London, 1721, and Letters to Serena, London, 1704.
Hegel, Georg, The Philosophy of History, Hackett Publishing Co., 1988.
Wordsworth, William, The Prelude, a Parallel Text, Penguin Books, 1996.
Whitman, Walt, Leaves of Grass, Penguin Books, 1997.
Ernst Haeckel, The Riddle of the Universe, Prometheus Books, Buffalo, 1992.
Robinson Jeffers, The Collected Poetry, Stanford University Press, 1989.
Calaprice, Alice, The Quotable Einstein, Princeton University Press, Princeton, 1996.
Lawrence, D. H., The Universe and Me, Henry Taylor, New York, 1935.

4. The Divine Universe
Otto, Rudolf, The Idea of the Holy, trs John Harvey, Oxford University Press, New York, 1968.

Hume, David, Dialogues Concerning Natural Religion, Oxford University Press, New York, 1994.

Hawking, Stephen, A Brief History of Time, Bantam Doubleday Dell, 1998.

Carl Sagan, Pale Blue Dot, Brilliance Corporation, 1994.

Guth, Allan, The Inflationary Universe, Helix Books, 1998.

Smolin, Lee, The Life of the Cosmos, Oxford University Press, 1998.

Per Bak, How Nature Works, Oxford University Press, Oxford, 1997.

Dennet, Daniel, Darwin's Dangerous Idea, Penguin Books, London 1995.

Dawkins, Richard, The Blind Watchmaker, Penguin Books, London, 1988

Barrow, John, & Tipler, Frank, The Anthropic Cosmological Principle, Oxford University Press, 1988.

5. Sacred Nature

Regenstein, Lewis, Replenish the Earth, SCM Press, London, 1991.

McGaa, Ed, Mother Earth Spirituality, Harper San Francisco, 1990.

Miller, Lee, From the Heart: Voices of the American Indian, Vintage Books, 1996.

Lovelock, James, Gaia, Gaia Books, London, 1991.

Goodenough, Ursula, The Sacred Depths of Nature, Oxford University Press, 1998.

Stewart, Ian, Life's Other Secret, John Wiley, London and New York, 1998.

E. O. Wilson, The Diversity of Life, W. W. Norton, 1993.

Cohen, Michael, Reconnecting with Nature, Project Nature Connect, Friday Harbor, Washington, 1995.

Roszak, Theodore, Ecopsychology, Sierra Club Books, San Francisco, 1995.

6. Ethics.

MacIntyre, Alasdair, A Short History of Ethics, Macmillan, 1966.

Singer, Peter, Animal Liberation, Avon Books, 1991.

Stone, Christopher, Earth and Other Ethics, Harper & Row, New York, 1987

Leopold, Aldo, A Sand County Almanach, Oxford University Press, New York, 1968.

Sessions, George, ed, Deep Ecology for the 21st Century, Shambala, Boston, 1995.

United Nations, International Covenant on Civil and Political Rights, and International Covenant on Economic, Social and Cultural Rights, United Nations, New York, 1966.

7. Ritual, meditation and mysticism.

Ayensu, Edward and Whitfield, Philip, The Rhythms of Life, Marshall Editions, London 1982.

Devall, Bill and Sessions, George, Deep Ecology, Peregrine Smith Books, Salt Lake City, 1985.

Ian Hutton, Stations of the Sun, Oxford University Press, Oxford & New York, 1996.

Albery, Nicholas, The Natural Death Handbook, Natural death centre, London, 1997.

Kabat-Zinn, Jon, Full Catastrophe Living, Dell Publishing, New York, 1990.

Woods, Richard, Understanding Mysticism, Image Books, New York, 1980.

Roberts, Elizabeth and Amidon, Elias, Earth Prayers, Harper San Francisco, 1991.

Mosley, Ivo, Earth Poems, Harper San Francisco, 1996.

8. Controversies

Rey, Georges, Contemporary Philosophy of Mind, Blackwell, Oxford, 1997.

Churchland, Paul, Matter and Consciousness, MIT Press, Cambridge Massachusetts, 1988.

Popper, Karl and Eccles, John, The Self and Its Brain, Routledge and Kegan Paul, London and Boston, 1977.

De Chardin, Teilhard, The Phenomenon of Man, Harper Collins, 1975.

Fox, Matthew, Original Blessings, Bear & Company, Santa Fe, 1983.

Head, Joseph and Cranston, Sylvia, The Phoenix Fire Mystery, Point Loma Publications, 1994.

Blackmore, Susan, Dying to Live, Grafton, London, 1993.

Williamson, John B., and Schneidman, Edwin, Death: Current Perspectives, Mayfield Publishing Company, 1995.

LaVergne, TN USA
11 January 2010
169611LV00008B/66/A